Becoming Italian

Chapter & Verse from an Italian American Girl

Linda Dini Jenkins

Jenkins, Linda Dini

Becoming Italian: Chapter & Verse from an Italian
American Girl / Linda Dini Jenkins.
p. 136

ISBN: 978-1-7365974-0-8

"Holding Up Our Half of the Sky at the End of the Twentieth
Century" first appeared in *South Florida Poetry Review*

"Tomato Knife" first appeared in *Voices in Italian Americana*
(VIA)

"Errands" first appeared in *Ovunque Siamo* (New Italian
American Writing)

Special photography by Jim Ognibene

Cover design and interior layout by Carolyn McGuire

The cover font is Italian in origin, too — Spira — apparently first used in Venice by Johannes and Vindelinus de Spira
for Cicero's Epistolae ad familiares in 1469.

TRAVEL
ITALY
the *Write Way*

To Clemente and Maria

The certificate reads:

THE CITY OF NEW YORK.
DEPARTMENT OF HEALTH.

STATE OF NEW YORK

No. of Certificate 13005

CERTIFICATE AND RECORD OF MARRIAGE

(Groom) Clemente Lini and (Bride) Maria Corazza

	Groom		Bride
Residence	412 - 20th St.		196 - 20th St.
Age	30		25
Color	White		White
Single, Widowed or Divorced	Widowed		single
Occupation	Laborer		
Birthplace	Italy		Italy
Father's Name	Ferdinande		Carmine
Mother's Maiden Name	Gabrielle Estere		Maria D'Angelo
Number of Marriage	first		first

I hereby certify that the above-named groom and bride were joined in Marriage by me, in accordance with the Laws of the State of New York, at _____ (Street/Church), in the Borough of _____, City of New York, this _____ of NOV 11 1917, 19__

Witnesses to the Marriage: Cecta Larch, Margherita Terano

Signature of person performing the Ceremony / Official Station: DEPUTY CITY CLERK

Residence: 137 EAST 30th Street

Ancestry

Not clotted cream or leg of lamb
Not goose or pudding, but
Lasagna and eggplant and mini sfogliatelle

Not crackers with Stilton and sherry
But homemade wine from mismatched juice glasses,
And after, a caffe coretto and amaro

You ask me why I ignore my English side
Well, buddy, this is why: a big juicy meatball
Trumps a dry, crumbly scone every time

Table of Contents

Part One: *i gentori e i nonni*

Part Two: *la figlia*

Part One:

i gentori e i nonni

Preface

Senta. Here's the way my novel was going to start. A friend convinced me that fiction was the only way to tell this story.

Fiction is not what I do, but I booked myself a hotel room in midtown Manhattan one January and wrote. And wrote. I got a little distracted by the world-class nor'easter that pelted the city that weekend, but I also managed to pump out four poems and this chapter start:

'I finally know what I want to do.'

Those are the words her mother spoke. She was dead within two weeks. It was the central line talking, the manic bravado of the morphine drip. Her mother was 64 years old.

When her mother died, Gina was in her fortieth year, suffering the effects of two failed relationships and floundering in her career. Even worse, the city that she'd loved all her life had begun to go bad on her.

Gina Marie Clare Liberatore knew that her days in New York City were numbered. The '80s had been an exhilarating ride. She'd had a decent career in advertising that ended just shy of the era of mega mergers and 22-year-old MBAs who thought they had all the answers. There was enough sex and drugs and partying to make her feel part of something. And there was New York itself: hub of the universe, center of the world, blah, blah, blah. By the time the '90s came around, it all started to not make sense anymore.

Two of the last sane things Gina had done just before it all blew up was to leave her eight-year relationship with the Harvard guy who couldn't stop working long enough to realize that she was pretty terrific, and to apply for a place at a writers' conference in Vermont. She dusted off a few old poems and submitted them. A few weeks later she got the news that she'd been accepted.

Once she'd gotten settled in her new refrigerator-box-sized apartment downtown, things got bad for her mother. A suspected UTI turned out to be much worse. It only took two months for the cancer to do its work. Gina was devastated. First, because her mother was so young, and second, because of those words, "I finally know what I want to do." Her mother would never get the chance. And Gina, now alone, had never been able to honestly say the same thing herself.

Sure, it's a thinly veiled biographical piece. Sure, what happens here really happened. Sure, these words from my mother stuck with me for another 10 years, until I finally went to Italy for the first time and my life changed in ways I could never have imagined. Not enough to become a writer of fiction, but in ways much more important.

Andiamo.

• • •

1949.

The only child of an Italian American father and a very American mother, I was born in Freeport, New York, the waterfront village where my mother's family had lived for a few hundred years. In 1956, my father moved us seven miles from Freeport to the "country" — Massapequa — which is also the hometown of Ron Kovic, Jerry Seinfeld, and the Baldwin brothers, whose father was a gym teacher at Massapequa High School.

As other half-Italian children can attest, the "Italian" side dominates. The others simply don't have a chance. There's the great food (vast quantities), the holidays (so many), the slavish attention to *la famiglia*, the volume (a little on the loud side), the non-verbal communication (an entire language of nods, shrugs and gestures) and the myriad superstitions. But where I differ from most other Italian kids is that I was not raised Roman Catholic.

In fact, on Surrey Lane where I grew up, there was just one Jewish family and only two Protestant families among the 30-odd houses. We were outnumbered. We had no catechism classes to attend, no mid-week confessions, and no weekend religious retreats to bind us together. As kids, we were outsiders.

My father, at age 14, youngest son of two Italian Catholic immigrants, crashed a Presbyterian dance one night and met my mother, aged 12. They were never apart after that, except for a few years when my sailor father served in the South Pacific during WWII.

It was not easy for them. My mother's mother wildly disapproved of the match, having deep suspicions about both Italians and Catholics which, in the 1930s and '40s, was pretty common. Hundreds of Italians were declared "enemy aliens" during World War II and were placed in internment camps. Back in Freeport, my grandmother made my father's life difficult for most of his marriage.

Or my father's mother seemed to always know that her Frankie would not marry an Italian girl and have a traditional Italian life. In their own way, both my parents brought a sense of loss or disappointment to their families.

Italian Catholic family on one side. German Catholic family (by marriage) on the other side. For a while I was even considered illegitimate. I'm told that rustling up some godparents was a chore.

So why am I telling you all this?

To show you how much some things have changed. And then again, how much they haven't. And to try to understand what it took for me to take a stand for my Italian-ness.

For me to start becoming Italian . . .

Goo-gootz

The goo-gootz are taking over the garden again
Light green, dark green, striped or no
Bumpy yellow long things
Indian club-sized vegetables that I transform
Into stratas and soup
Stuff their blossoms with savory ricotta and herbs
Grill until they're charred and sweet
Fling over pasta with fresh tomatoes and basil
Hand out to curious neighbors
Expecting them to love these jewels the way I do
The goo-gootz of my little garden
The goo-gootz of my roots

I Wasn't Always Italian

I am always reading about Italy, about traveling to Italy, about living in Italy, and about the stories of ex-pats in Italy. A few years ago, I came across a book called, *Were You Always an Italian? Ancestors and Other Icons of Italian America* by the journalist Maria Laurino. Here is Laurino writing about her interview with former New York Governor Mario Cuomo:

> "'Were you always an Italian?' Mario Cuomo asked me some years ago.

> "His sententious question captured my own ethnic ambivalence. Cuomo was sitting in the ceremonial governor's office, a large, rarely used room in Albany restored to its ornate nineteenth-century splendor. His feet rested on a mahogany desk polished to a shiny luster, and he was leaning a little too far back to look entirely comfortable. To him, 'being' Italian meant understanding the Mezzogiorno [southern Italian] culture; being Italian meant overcoming the urge to hide the impoverished land of your ancestry.

> "With childlike guilt, I shook my head no."

He then goes on to talk about what he calls "ethnic self-hate." While I never experienced anything that strong, I was not Italian in public. What does that even mean? It means bologna sandwiches with mayo on white bread for school lunches. It means my father bought me clothes that he described as "classy": box-pleated wool skirts from a pre-preppy store called Villager, with matching cardigan sweaters and knee socks to go with some shiny oxblood penny loafers. Muted colors — beige, navy, brown — so I wouldn't stand out too much. Other girls in school wore clothes from Villager, too. The really popular girls. Skulking through the corridors, I nodded nervously at them. They seemed legit. Why did I feel like such a fraud?

When I was 15, Dad took me to weekly dermatology appointments for my acne-prone skin: ultra-violet treatments in the office and harsh soap at home. We made visits to the Clinique counter at Macy's, where he dropped obscene amounts of money on lotions and potions for me. Grooming was all important, and he patterned this for me by being fastidious in his dress and by carefully arranging his thick black pompadour hair each morning. Image was everything.

How did I not see that this was Daddy's way to live *la bella figura*? Well, there was that, but there was also this: Being above criticism was how you avoided it. Always look above reproach, don't speak 'til you're spoken to, work harder than anybody else, take the crumbs when they're offered to you . . . this was how to live a life without making waves. And making waves was disastrous if you were raised to think you couldn't — or shouldn't — swim.

Dad designed my bedroom so that it sparkled with pickled faux-wood paneling throughout. He installed built-in shelves for my many (even back then) books, a nook for my desk, and a place for my all-important music. Over my bed were two telling reproductions –

not maps of Italy or family portraits. No, over my bed was a duo of the most non-Italian girls in the world: Renoir's "A Girl with a Watering Can" and "Madame Georges Charpentier and her Children." What was I supposed to do with that information literally hanging over my head? I knew they weren't me. But who was I?

I listened to my *nonno* speak Italian to my father, and heard my father, remarkably, talking back. I shouldn't have been surprised; Italian was my father's first language. But when I asked them to teach me, they both said, with a little regret, that they didn't speak Italian – "only a dialect." They even undervalued their local dialect, believing that because they didn't speak Dante's "Florentine" Italian, that it was somehow not a real language.

At grandpa's house in Freeport, I stood next to the stove on a little wooden stool, which I have with me to this day, and watched my *nonna* make red sauce and meatballs. A flowered oilcloth covering on the table held a big shallow bowl of wrin-

kled black olives in oil, a few garlic cloves thrown in among the parsley. That's how the house smelled. On Sundays, my grandparents' bed was covered by a sheet holding the freshly made pasta, drying, being readied for the meal.

The wine cellar was just that: the old stone dirt-floor cellar where grandpa made his red wine. Two big oak barrels sat up on a concrete pediment. I thought it was the worst wine imaginable, so bitter, but it was his and we drank it from Howdy Doody jelly jar glasses together every other Sunday, when he came for lunch. And there was his garden outside, where tomatoes and peppers and escarole and herbs of all kinds were grown, every bit of it either consumed by us then or canned and stacked in glass jars under the cellar staircase for the winter. And there was the pergola behind the garage where we spent summer afternoons under the grapevines, talking and eating at the rustic table.

But back in Massapequa, Mom, Dad and I (and Grandma) lived in a white cape house with ridiculous pink shutters (my mother's favorite color) and a basketball hoop. Dad worked early hours at a defense plant and was gone before 7:00 a.m. He usually took me to school on the way to work, and most days I had to wait for a custodian to come over and unlock the door for me. I wonder what he thought about this shy girl, coming to school alone at such an ungodly hour.

My Dad wore a coat and tie to work. I wore my Villager outfits to school and played violin, wrote poetry, and was an introverted nerd caught between two worlds.

In those days, Dad hadn't yet graduated from high school, but he was working on his GED, and then his associate's degree from the State University of New York. He worked hard to get into a solid middle-management staff position, sacrificing sleep and hours with his family. He learned how to handle every authority figure who tried to diminish him, but it took its toll. He took early retirement at the age of 55 because he was tired of fighting. He spent the remainder of his life trying to be happy, but he missed work and lived in fear of what would become of him and my mother.

Italian was the last thing the kids at school or at my liberal Methodist church would have labeled me. Teachers mispronounced my name, and my ethnicity was uncertain. Kids with names like Tedesco, Camissa, Camarrata, and Corradino were much easier to label; I was something of a mystery, despite brown hair and brown eyes and a name that ended in a vowel.

Massapequa was known as "Matzah-Pizza" in those days. If you weren't Jewish, you were Italian.

I was neither, it seemed.

Black and White, 1952

Anna Maria and Josefina
Maria and Josie
Cotton flowered house dresses
Aprons and sensible black shoes
Standing by the kitchen door
Holding on to each other
Squinting at the sun
Laughing at something long-forgotten
Wiry black and silver curls
Falling on their foreheads
A Kodak Brownie recording the scene

Nonna and Josie
Can I crawl inside there with you?
Is there any room?
There is so much I want to know

Grandma

I have no idea who Josie was. A sister? A cousin? A friend she came over with on the boat? I can't say.

Same with Millie. Millie was my father's godmother (*cumare*), married to Virgilio, who my grandfather worked for. Were they related? Did they come from the same village in the old country? No idea.

When I asked my father about *nonna*, he said her name was Anna Maria DeAngelis. But when my husband Tim and I did some digging, we found that her marriage certificate says Anna Maria Iacovazza. She is the mother of Francesco and Ferdinando (my father and uncle), but apparently my *nonno* was married before. His marriage license says he was a widower. My father told me that *nonno* had lost his first wife and child in childbirth. In Italy? In America? Was his first wife also Anna Maria?

In doing the research for my dual citizenship (which at this rate will take me the rest of my life), I learned that she came from a small village – Montano Antilia – near Salerno, in the province of Campania. She was born in 1893 and came to the United States as a young woman in the early part of the twentieth century. I have seen some evidence that Iacovazza is her name and that DeAngelis is her mother's name (Italian women typically keep their father's name, not their husband's name, which makes genealogy a bit tricky.) The story is still unfolding . . .

While my English-Irish-German-Cocker Spaniel grandmother (how my father described her) was a constant presence in our lives, *Nonna* Maria was not. She died when I was about five years old. It seems silly to say that she taught me how to cook. But she did teach me that cooking was important, was an art form, was survival, was nurturing, and I did see her making more red sauce in my five years than most non-Italians see in a lifetime.

She stood me up on a little wooden four-legged stool and had me watch her smash the garlic, sweat the onions, strain the tomatoes from the garden, and make a magic sauce that formed the basis for a week's worth of meals. If *nonno* had a good week, there might be a little beef or sausage in the sauce. My father used to say that you could eat his mother's meatballs on Friday.

Nonna Maria was not well. I remember her being almost as wide as she was tall. When I got a little older, I learned that she had both heart disease and diabetes. But she was a formidable woman. She never went to school, was designated "illiterate" when she arrived at Ellis Island, but she was nobody's fool. Shopkeepers feared her. Bankers were astounded by her. My father

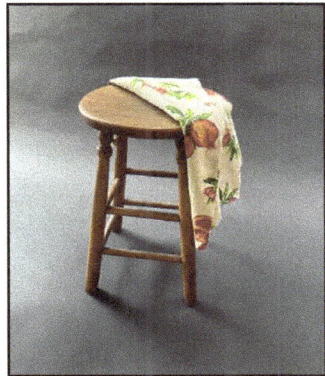

admired her but was still a little embarrassed by her old country ways and deep suspicion that everybody was trying to put one over on her. And let's face it, they probably were.

I remember her in her flowered dresses bending over the plants in the garden, harvesting green peppers, pole beans, parsley, basil, and tomatoes. I remember her stash of canning jars on the shelves under the cellar stairs that kept the family in fresh beans and sauce all winter. I remember holding my breath when she picked up the round loaf of bread just before lunch and, holding it chest level, drew the knife to her body to cut it. To this day, I have never seen an American cut bread like that.

I remember her whole body shaking with laughter as her two boys told her stories of their work and their very different American lives. She was always a foreigner in this country, with wiry Mediterranean hair and a thick accent, and she didn't make it here past her fifties.

I long to hear her side of the story. What she suffered, how she got here, who she travelled with, what she gave up, and whether she had any regrets.

I am Italian because of her and her husband, because of my father and uncle, and because of the family they created, and which nurtured me.

Errands

He was at the mercy of his mother,
Strong fingered hand gripping his little boy paw
Pulling him down the street to run errands.

Back then, there was still the butcher and the baker
And the vegetable man to visit, all along the streets of
Sunset Park. She bargained while he cringed, hoping

Just once she would pay what was asked. Hoping just
Once she would not reach into the oil-stained paper bag
In which she kept her money, the garlic scented money,

Waiting for the inevitable discount, leaving satisfied
And just a little smug. He used to say that she could
Calculate compound interest in her head, this peasant girl

From the old country, who never saw the inside
of a schoolhouse.
Still, the child in him wilted as they walked down
20th Street,
Past the banker and the milkman and the fruit
vendor, Daddy
Aching to be nothing more
than American.

Brutta Figura

I am seventeen, about to graduate from high school
My hair is severely chopped, a la Twiggy
Everybody is trying to get used to it
The boy next door has just moved to Florida with
his family
I am sure my last prospects for happiness went
with them
In an act of dramatic teen-age defiance and
self-mutilation
I cut off my hair

And I never told anybody this story before

Clemente

Grandpa comes over for lunch the Sunday before my high school graduation. Clemente can't quite wrap his head around this haircut. I remember that I had bought a "fall" to wear after realizing that this homage to Twiggy was not going to cut it under a graduation mortarboard. And then I have a thought. What if I switch back and forth from the really short hair to the hairpiece while *Nonno* Clemente was here? Will he notice?

After only two changes, he looks at me pleadingly and asks, "Wadda you do?" I take the fall off and show him my newly cropped hair and we all laugh. He says he even likes it, but to stop confusing him like that. Honesty. That was part of his charm.

It was special when he came for lunch. Usually Daddy cooked, and that was always good, a great relief from Mom's chicken steaks and boxed mac and cheese. He and Grandpa would talk in Italian while they worked in the garden – we grew lots of green peppers, and six-foot-tall tomato plants in the backyard, which needed re-stabilizing every couple of weeks. Summers were the best. A little glass of *vino* on the back patio was a guilty pleasure for a young girl.

Clemente bought me my first bicycle. It was a black Royce Union skinny tire racing bike with its own air pump, and it was propped up under the Christmas tree one year — it was the most beautiful bike I had ever seen. And he always had a few dollars folded up neatly into the shallow pocket of his sweater vest, ready to give out to the grandchildren.

My grandfather was a gentle man, to my eyes, but when a man came around to the old Brooklyn neighborhood years before to offer "protection" to families and businesses, things changed. Some families succumbed to the pressure and paid. Clemente has the distinction of being one of the few to ever stand up to these thugs: this slim, soft-spoken bricklayer broke the legs of one of the guys (with a bat, so the story goes), and they never came back to bother him again.

Maybe the pressures of the neighborhood, combined with the Great Depression and the desire to assimilate, made Clemente decide to pack up his small family and move to the "country." Or maybe he just missed having a garden of his own. In any case, in 1935, he relocated the family to Freeport, New York about 40 miles away from Brooklyn. In truth, it was a world away. North Long Beach Avenue was a street of tidy little free-standing houses where you needed a car to get most anywhere. Clemente learned to drive. And he put his boys in school so they could learn English and become American.

He lost his second wife at a young age and remained a widower for the rest of his life, but he kept their little house in Freeport going, and their garden going, until the end. Clemente loved to watch wrestling on the black and white TV he had in the living room, and he smoked a pipe, whose smell was the best thing in the world. He liked his coffee with Four Roses Whiskey in it (*coretto*) and needed a piece of bread in his left hand to eat lunch and dinner (he would *fare la scarpetta*, make the little shoe, with the slice of bread to get up all the sauce).

He wore a hat: a grey fedora with a black band. He wore sweater vests and plaid shirts and corduroy trousers. He was never without a smile as long as I knew him, and I never heard him curse in English. There was a curious dent in his nose about one third of the way down from his forehead. Daddy said that a hatchet came loose from a beam in the base-

ment ceiling and fell on Clemente's nose. Who knows? Another story was that a 23-year-old Clemente walked shoeless from his Tuscan village (San Casciano dei Bagni) to Naples in 1914, on the Mediterranean coast, to board the ship Perugia to come to America. Barefoot? Again, who knows?

We went back to Brooklyn once or twice a year. Some-times for a chaotic few hours to see the relatives who were still living in the old neighborhood. More often, to buy produce. Crates and crates of grapes for Grandpa's wine and bushels of big, white capped mushrooms for Dad's lasagna. There was a mysterious air about these trips – Mom didn't come – just me and Daddy and Grandpa. Doing Italian things.

When my father talked about the moon landing — he worked on the lunar module project — Clemente was skeptical. He said that he believed what he saw on television was a stage set in Bayonne, New Jersey. Space travel was something he could never quite believe, and who could blame him? It was perilous enough to travel from village to village where he came from. Why would anybody set their sights on the heavens?

Sometimes we'd drive to Jones Beach, and he'd show off the marvelous mosaic sea creatures he had made on the walkway of the Central Mall as part of the WPA. Clemente owned an almost metallic green Ford sedan, circa 1962, that he drove back and forth between Freeport and Massapequa, and Freeport and East Meadow, to visit his sons on alternate Sundays. He worked until he was 83 and dying of throat cancer. Mercifully, he went quickly, but I always regretted that he never got to meet Tim and that he never knew about my late passion for all things Italian.

I know he was proud of his sons and his grandchildren. All three of us kids graduated from college and we looked to all the world like we were Americans. One a teacher, one a pharmacist, and one . . . well, nobody really knew what I was going to be.

After the Funeral

For Clemente

You promised to dance at my wedding when
I was a child
but when I saw your thin frame placed upon the
bone-white bed
and felt your faint, beaten smile brush my face
I knew you would not and was afraid.

Had he lived
my father would have had to take him in,
another parent-child.

To feed him, he would have had to stuff
earth-colored mash down a plastic tube
passing through where his throat had been.

To ignore his humiliation would have been impossible.

After the funeral, we took a ride in the rain
my father and I
and went nowhere, wordlessly.

I feared this death the most:
afraid for my father
for the loss of the last of the last generation.

After the funeral
driving
the silence was the hardest thing to hear.

My Father's Story

Francesco Dini was born in
Brooklyn, New York on
May 23, 1922, the second
son of Clemente Dini and
Maria Iacovazza. Clemente
was born in Tuscany, in a
village near Siena; Maria
was born in Campania, in a
village not far from Salerno.
They met in Brooklyn. Their
first son, Ferdinando, was
my uncle, two years older
than my father.

Frank Dini lived in a row house in Sunset Park,
Brooklyn until he was 12 years old. He didn't talk
much about it, other than that he lived close to his
father's friends and co-workers. One of the ways you
got to come over from the old country was to be sponsored for work by someone who was already here.
Clemente came to work for Joe Pizzo, a man from
the old neighborhood, as a bricklayer and mason. So,
along with Dinis and Pizzos, there were Cacciolis and
Muros and Ceccarellis, all names that my father grew
up with.

Sunset Park in those days was an immigrant ghetto,
so there was little need to speak much English unless
you were the boss and had to interact with "American"
clients. Where my father lived, Italian was spoken in
the home and in school and life was pretty much as it

would have been in Italy except, eventually, for running water. *Nonna* loved telling about the toilet facilities — the "backhous-a" — that they endured.

It was a familiar scene: long Sunday lunches, lots of family breezing in and out of the apartment, women doing all the housework and cooking and child rearing, men away for the day at hard labor, the *fruttivendolo* driving his horse-drawn cart through the neighborhood streets, the butcher and baker and cheese maker just around the corner.

By the time my father was 12, his family had moved out to the suburbs to try to become Americans. But it wasn't that easy.

Italians had accents, they were dark-skinned, they smelled like garlic, they were mostly poor, and they had a reputation for being criminal-minded. Worse than that, however — they were Catholic. Smells and rituals. A foreign language. Fear and obligation and terrifying images. A faith that was not well received in a suburban WASP America that was trying to pull itself out of the morass of the war to end all war, even if Italians had fought alongside them. And then there was the Pope — a higher authority than any president, which was deemed un-American. Like a lot of first-generation Italians, Frankie had a hard time.

He never told me much about his school days, other than being teased for not speaking English right away. He quickly learned and fell in with a group of guys, most of whom remained his friends for life. Knowing them as I did as grown-ups, I assume there were a lot of stories that he chose not to tell me. The one he told over and over again, however, was about the night their gang (the Korkas) decided to crash a dance at the local Presbyterian Church. It was there that he met a shy 12-year-old named Dolly; eight years later they were married.

But before that happened, Dad quit high school to go to work and then joined the US Navy to fight in World War II. Mom quit school too, to work in the same defense plant that my Dad worked in (Grumman Aircraft Engineering Corporation, as it was called then). She worked the blueprint machine while Dad fought it out in the South Pacific. When he came home in 1944, they were married and went together to Daytona Beach for his final months of service.

Back in New York, they moved into my mother's mother's house in Freeport — a small two-bedroom apartment on the second floor. Grandma and Grandpa Raynor lived downstairs in the house that Grandpa had built. It was a big, dark-shingled foursquare on a corner lot, with a screened-in porch, cherry and apple trees in the yard, and a big barn in the back. I came along after five years and it was a good place to grow up for a while.

I was too young to appreciate the stress my father was under, trying to raise a young family and build a career, while being constantly belittled by his mother-in-law, who never forgave her daughter for marrying an Italian. My father put up with this through two houses and 28 years of her living under his roof and being flat-out supported by him. She was an impossible woman to live with, all passive aggressive four-foot-ten of her. My father, the lapsed Catholic, should have been sainted for the miracle of not killing her at least once during this time.

After the Navy, Dad went back to Grumman; Mom never worked outside the home again after I was born. Through the late 1940s and early 1950s he moved from the "shop floor" to become an engineering assistant and then, encouraged by his superiors, went to school and came out as a hydraulics/pneumatics engineer. Dad was conscientious, but not confident. Olive skinned and raven haired, he couldn't hide his ethnicity; with an English-Irish mother, I was easier to assimilate.

By 1956, racial tensions had reached a boiling point in our little community. We were the only white family left on the block, but my grandmother didn't want to leave the house her husband built for her all those years ago. When I turned six, I needed a police escort to my elementary school. We were receiving threats from the neighbors and I was regularly accused of stealing toys from the kids who had up 'til then been my only friends. Dad felt we had to get out, and so we moved to Massapequa after the school year was over. A few months later, reluctantly, grandma came, too, and we began our new life in the "new" suburbs.

Dad worked his way up to be a Staff Assistant for one of the Vice Presidents, a prestigious position that required all kinds of time and political savvy. But even as a teen-ager I could tell that the job was killing him. During the 1960s Grumman expanded into other areas: boats, private jets, trucks. The high point for Dad was working on the Apollo Lunar Module that got Neil Armstrong and Buzz Aldrin to the moon in 1969. He also received a patent for an air conditioning coupling unit that Grumman called the "Dini-Flex." Dad got the press, but Grumman got the money.

By the time he left in 1978, my Dad said disgustedly that the bigwigs would make oatmeal if they thought it could turn a profit. He took their meager early retirement package and moved to Florida with my mother; they wanted to be near some of those old high school friends who had all moved down a few years before.

Dad had a wicked sense of humor. King of the one-liners, he had something to say about everything and everybody. I remember times in traffic when, if the person in front of him didn't speed off at the changing light, he would yell: "What are you waiting for, buddy? A color you like?" Or when he heard some pounding and unintelligible song blasting from someone else's car radio and would say: "Ooooh, it must be a love song."

Back in the days of door-to-door salesmen, Dad answered a knock one Sunday afternoon. I heard the pitch on the other side of the door from a man trying to strong-arm Dad into buying a nice piece of jewelry for his wife. Without missing a beat, I saw my Dad break down and tell him that his wife had just passed away, that he'd love to if only he could . . . well, the man fled. Dad closed the door and we all practically fell on the floor with laughter.

When I was a kid, I howled at his made-up stories about "Joe Maddarazz" who made "Fatsamachasmazzeroni cheese." When I was a really little kid, he would sing *Abba Dabba Honeymoon* and *Inka-Dinka-Doo* to me in the bathtub. We shared a passion for *Mad Magazine*. I danced with my feet on his until I was too big to do so.

He was a great cook and a consummate entertainer. Friend to all the neighborhood kids, talented artist, very capable business writer – often quoting Machiavelli in his missives to top brass — he was an all-round creative guy. But he would only allow himself to go so far.

He internalized stress until it made him sick. Like so many of that generation, he overused alcohol until it did him harm. Something about his upbringing made him hold back, believe he had limits, put any kind of authority in front of his own. It made me angry and sad and it was a revelation to realize, years later, that I would run my professional life the same way, always feeling a little less than, always grateful to friends for leads, always beholden to anyone who would provide me with a paycheck.

Was this ethnic shame? I don't know. I do know that it was learned behavior. Holding back, not complaining until you were ready to explode, deferring to people you perceived to have better credentials, experience, pedigree, avoiding confrontation at any cost. But he saw boundaries that I cannot even imagine.

He was not the boy who survived the Sunset Park neighborhood in the 1930s, the one whose father had told the mob to go to hell. This funny, talented man spent his life being cautious and fearful, and readily accepted the back seat. In his last few years, under the influence of recovery and Parkinson's-related dementia, he became mean-spirited and filled with regret. It was one of the saddest times of my life.

Tomato Knife

The butcher block cutting board bleeds thin red water
and small yellow seeds as I slice a huge beefsteak
for sandwiches

Carefully, methodically, I bring the tiny serrated-edge
knife down
through the flesh again and again, the white
plastic handle fitting
snugly in my palm

This was my father's tomato knife; he used to say he
could make
slices so thin that you could read through them

In the tiny square kitchen of my childhood, it
came out
every summer evening, when we would harvest
ready fruit from the yard

I can see him still against the knotty-pine wall,
shoeless, sporting
cargo shorts, a sleeveless tee, an unlit Corona in
his mouth
showing off his skill like a surgeon

Once I saw him dance around the kitchen doing
blade magic
with white-capped mushrooms, with ripe plum
tomatoes, with
giant garlic bulbs and layered golden onions,
conjuring up
a perfect sauce in no time, pepper and cheese riding
on the surface olive oil

So I have taken this cheap artifact with me from
house to house
tucking it into my drawer, bringing it out from
time to time
when such precision is required

His younger strength is forged into it:
his bravado
his Italian
his hospitality

And I like to think that something of that remains
in my hand,
cutting into the past, letting the sweet juices flow

Cousins

I had four first cousins, a ridiculously small family for an Italian girl. Two strawberry blonde ones on my mother's side and two dark-haired, dark-eyed Italian ones on my father's side. Then there was me.

At Christmas, whatever my blonde girl cousin got in pink, I got in blue. Still, I was closer to her because she was just a year younger than I was, while my dark-haired Italian cousin was four years older, which seemed like a huge gap at the time. The two boys were, well, boys. They were younger, in any case.

In 2017, while I was leading a tour in Italy, my cousin Freddie died of complications from a liver transplant and leukemia. I was devastated. The group could tell, and they toasted him every night at our dinners in Venice.

Most holidays were celebrated at our house. We had BBQs in the summer and huge meals for the big deal food holidays. Always an ethnic mix of food. Turkey with all the trimmings . . . plus lasagna. Easter ham . . . with eggplant parmesan. There might have been a few season-appropriate pies for dessert, but the main event was always colorful, decadent miniature pastries from the Italian bakery: cream puffs, *cannoli*, *sfogliatelle*, rum cakes, and *struffoli*. It was high-calorie confusion, to be sure.

My younger cousin and I went to the same college, so we saw each other a lot. Besides, her father (my mother's twin brother) was a great friend to me, even though he broke his family's heart and ended up dying an early death from alcohol and emphysema. It wasn't until I was grown and living in New York City that I became close to my Italian cousin.

I was living with a guy on the Upper East Side and got a call that she and her husband and another couple were on their annual President's Day long weekend in the city and would we like to join them. We said yes, and an almost-annual tradition was born, lasting through the death of her husband and the break-up of my relationship and into the next relationships for both of us. We had great fun reminiscing about our parents, our childhoods, how we survived, and how we were living in the world in the crazy 1980s.

A few years ago, after we had both been to Italy several times (but never together), I told her that I was thinking about applying for dual citizenship and getting an Italian passport. She got very quiet. I could see that she was choosing her words carefully, but what she said totally blew me away.

"How could you do that?" she asked. *"It was so hard for grandpa to come here and make a living. And all he wanted to do was raise two boys who would have the advantage of being American."*

Her answer took my breath away. It sounded like wanting Italian citizenship was a betrayal of everything that our grandparents had gone through all those years ago. I had never thought about it this way. In fact, I rather thought that Clemente would be pleased by my decision. I have been thinking about my cousin's response ever since, and about why we came at this from such different places.

Maybe with four years on me, she was privy to more talk in her home about Italy and what drove our grandfather to leave when he did. My father was also younger than her father, so maybe the conversations just didn't trickle down to us.

When I asked my father to come to Italy with me and Tim in 2001, he declined, although he thought about it for a little while. Then the objections came. *You shouldn't go, either. You don't know the language . . . you don't know anybody there . . . you don't know the roads, the towns, blah, blah, blah.*

Maybe getting dual citizenship just seemed "un-American." But more than wonder why my cousin reacted the way she did, I've been trying to think about why this step is so important for me.

From the just first time I set foot on Italian soil, I felt at home. It just made sense. Something about the air and the clean water draws me in, every time. As do the slower pace of the countryside, the attention to food and wine, and all the things they grow and consume. I love that Italians live and eat according to the seasons.

I am impressed that, once you get out of the big cities, there is both a lack of overconsumption and a still-tight hold onto traditional ways of doing things. And I am fascinated by the Christian rituals which have their roots deep in pagan festivals and superstitions, like Cocullo and its vipers on San Domenico's feast day and Gubbio's Festa dei Ceri. Every little village has its own interpretations, its own food festivals (*sagre*), its own take on what community means.

My home in Sulmona, in the Abruzzo region, is in the Valle Peligna surrounded by massive, usually snow-capped mountains. It is the greenest area in Europe, with both regional and national parks and tons of wildlife. Walk to the main piazza in Sulmona, look up and take in the scene. The fountain. Those mountains. And then realize that you're standing under Frederick II's 13th-century aqueduct, practically within spitting distance of five churches.

I love that people say hello to you there. *"Buon giorno"* or *"Salve."* I've tried saying hello to strangers in the States. It usually flops. You get either nothing or a suspicious look.

History is everywhere: in the fountains, in the churches, in the architecture of the *piazze*. It's in the pageantry of each village's special moments . . . the Easter processions, the barefoot barrel races, the *palio*, the Renaissance *giostra*, the outdoor movies and concerts, the markets. All history, all pageantry of one sort or another. Even food is pageantry.

Come late afternoon-early evening, there's the *passeggiata*, when the whole town turns out for a walk up and down the *corso*, greeting one another, catching up on the day's news, enjoying a *gelato* or an *aperitivo*. *Nonne* walking arm-in-arm, little dogs barking endlessly, children playing or riding their *biciclette*, men doffing their hats to one another, finally settling into the bars for a whisky or a spritz.

It's a little Fellini-esque. And it puts everything into perspective.

Our grandparents left the South mostly because the entrenched feudal agricultural society was collapsing and work was disappearing. There was no future for most young men, so they left for a better life. Some of them for just a short time, some forever.

We are not naïve. Italy has its problems, both political and economic, and in some ways, the same thing is happening now. 2022 unemployment rates in Southern Italy are projected to reach nearly 20%, and most young people nowadays leave for careers up north or abroad.

Still, the small-town life is the life that calls to me. I want dual citizenship to declare that these are my roots, this is what my grandparents had to miss as a result of their very difficult decision, this is what was denied them but it will not be denied to me.

The process is daunting, mostly because talking family history was not a popular pastime in my house. I've finally hired a service to track everything down for me. Fingers crossed, some day – if the consulates are ever fully operational again -- I may be the incredibly proud owner of an Italian passport.

I hope my cousin will understand.

I See Clemente Sitting
on a Bench Just Outside
Piazza Garibaldi, Sulmona

What would he think, me in this little mountain town?
The music-minded, poetry writing city girl,
far from home?

I think it might seem right: the men in their
pressed pants
And cotton shirts, sweater vests and, sometimes, a hat

Smiling, despite great losses
Strong spirits in once-strong bodies

I think he would study the piazza
The perfect stone arches of the aqueduct
Note how the cobbles were set, would pause
For the call of the campanile and perhaps fill his pipe

Wistfully, before joining the others on the bench to
watch life pass
By slowly and declaring it, eventually, mostly good

I see Clemente, who worked in brick and stone
and tile all his life —
Clemente, who was father, husband,
grandfather, wholly
Italian in a sometime hostile America

I think he would approve of this place, loving this
Madre Majella as I do, with her ever-present poppies
With her wild beasts and trails and tumbled ruins

I think the wine and figs and olives would please
him, too
And he would be happy for me, the grandchild least
likely to come,
The one who has found her heart here

Dolly's Choice

I was driving my mother to a mall in Florida, because that's what we did. I was 30 years old and had come down from New York for a visit. It was hot. It was almost always hot, except when you came down in January hoping for hot. Then you had to scrape frost off the car windows in the morning.

But on this particular hot day, Mom and I were talking. Before long, she said the words that still make me reel 40 years later. She looked over at me and said:

You know, I've been mad at you since you were five years old.

I nearly drove off the road. Seriously. What could I possibly have done at age five? How could I have offended her so deeply? What awful thing could I have said that, as an adult, she could not process, ignore, or forgive? I came up empty. Nada. Zilch. Zero. After regaining the wheel, I asked her what she meant.

When mom was angry, she breathed through her nostrils, hard, like a dragon. She did this then. She told me that one day we were down in her mother's kitchen. She asked me to do something (she couldn't remember what) and I grabbed her by the knee and kicked her in the ankle. I was having a temper tantrum, and she had been mad at me for 25 years for this.

I had no idea what to say. *I'm sorry* would have been disingenuous, since neither one of us could even remember the circumstances. *I was just a little kid* seemed perfectly obvious. *What did you do then?* seemed beside the point. So we both just continued on in silence. It was never resolved. I was never redeemed. We went on like that for another 10 years, until she died.

Dorothy Louise Raynor Dini was a very unhappy woman.

The girl child in a pair of twins born at home in 1924 to a then-ancient 36-year-old mother, Dolly was always second best. She got her brother's hand-me-down bike and toys, she was assigned the bulk of the household chores, she had to stay at home when he could go out with his friends, and so on. And on. The male privilege thing. But young Dolly had a surprising rebellious streak.

She ran away from home when she was 15 – underage – to take a summer job at a resort in Saratoga Springs, New York. She jumped on a bus and was met by a friend who had paved the way with a part-time job for her and a shared room. She served breakfast to high rollers and temporarily escaped life with a petulant mother who frequently blamed her daughter for the difficult birth that "almost tore her insides out." She was the last twin out. It was her fault.

By that time, she had already started to smoke and drink. But these weren't her only rebellions. At age 20, she stunned her family by marrying a first-generation Italian American. At age 25, she gave birth to me, but she never had another child — an unusual choice in those days — despite my father's desire to have more children. In her thirties and forties, she gave more to Girl Scouts than she did to her family: camping, weekly meetings, road trips to national scouting events — even after I was long out of the organization myself.

My mother was ill-equipped to be a parent. She always saw me as a threat to her relationship with her husband and played that out in ugly ways. Competition. Jealousy. Constant belittling. Passive aggressive behavior. Casting doubt. Knocking me off my pegs whenever possible. At Girl Scout summer camp, I actually asked the head honcho — who knew my family well — if I had been adopted. I felt so removed from my mother that this was the only explanation that my ten-year-old brain could come up with.

I would sometimes come home after school to find my mother stretched out on her bed and I knew that Mommy had taken a phenobarbital to cope with Grandma again. Scotch and soda was her drink of choice, and she imbibed every night until bedtime. It was during these fugue states that I would hear her, incessantly, tell stories about how pretty, thin, smart, and successful everybody else's kids were. I tried to stay out of her way.

As a result, I married too soon and to the wrong man, simply to get out of the nuthouse. When I told her, eight years later, that we were getting divorced, she said to me — matter-of-factly and without one iota of concern — *I wondered how long that would take.* When, a few years after that, I got an acceptance to the prestigious Bread Loaf Writers Conference (a dream since college), she simply asked, *Oh, you mean that thing you have to pay for?*

I was never enough. Nothing I did was ever good enough. It's a tough way to grow up and it carries permanent scars. I wrote a poem once about how I was a "careful communicator," walking on eggs throughout my childhood, having to be prepared with facts and charts at the dinner table before I dared open my mouth. There was no making a mistake. There was no being wrong. There was no taking risks. Failure of any kind was lethal. She lived for the "gotcha."

I cannot put together the young woman my mother was with what she had become. My suspicion is that she probably married the wrong man, too, and that she never really wanted children. She was a life-long caretaker for her difficult mother, and she had found a way out by drinking and isolation. In that morphine-induced fog in which cancer patients often end their days, she told me that I was all she ever wanted. She also told me, on her death bed, that she finally knew what she wanted to do with her life.

Regret. It was palpable. I still believe today that it was her choice to die when she did, refusing any more radiation after just seven treatments.

The question lingers, though: what the hell could I have done to her as a five-year-old child to make her turn on me? To keep her mad at me for 25 years? I'll never know. The invisible child that I had become still tugs on my shirtsleeve sometimes. I wish I had an answer for her.

The Dream is Almost Always
Exactly the Same

I am running, I have been chased, to the edge
Of something, always with an unfathomable drop

Often, an unfamiliar ridge, where I stand,
wildly circling
My outstretched arms, cartoon style, on tip toes
—A real cliffhanger

Once, on the lip of a steel girdered future high rise,
Like in the old photo of those men with their lunch pails
In 1932 at 30 Rock, and I do not know how I got there

At times, I am on the wing of the plane taking
me to Rome
Frantic, beltless, nothing below me, *niente, solo le nuvole*

The drop, the potential plunge, comes back
again and again
And, from my horizontal position in the bed, I jump,
My knees straighten abruptly, trying to save
whatever is left
In my sweaty state and, at this point, I usually
kick the dog

I think of my mother, Dorothy, Dolly, and her
love for the risk
(Isn't it why she married my Italian father, after all?)

She was game for every rust bucket over a whirlpool,
Every tram or bridge over raging waters, every funicular
Chugging up a jagged mountain wall, every boat
under a waterfall

One afternoon, when her mother was napping,
she told me
To get in the car, that we were going for a drive
I was already 19 and home from college, but I got in

And we drove more than two hours each way to
Bear Mountain so that she could sit on the t-bar
Of the ski resort in summer in time to make it back
For supper so nobody would know we'd been away

Another time, it was off to Coney Island, where
she put me
In the front seat of the Bobsled ride so she could
relive some
Teen-age memory that was better than the ones she
was making now

Closer to home, she would drive us out to Stonybrook
To watch the wooden mechanical eagle on the
Post Office pediment
Flap its 20-foot wingspan on the hour
As it has done every day since 1941

This speed, this height, this danger — things my father
And I did not share with her; it was dizzying, foreign

These days, long after they both are gone, I wonder
Just what centripetal force held them together, why
They did not, at some point, simply break apart

Leaving me breathless, like Mom's death-defying
Coney Island Parachute Jump, like
The Wile E. Coyote cliffs of all my restless nights

Once Upon a Time in the Fifties

Excessive influence of the ladies' magazines
The perfect little sitcoms

New house, new cars
Doctor in his Avanti, peddling little pills

Frilly fruited aprons and high heels
Pink and grey tiled bathrooms with

Happy French Poodle wallpaper
The requisite neighborhood cocktail parties

— Martini at the door —
— Dinner on the table —

Post-war prosperity, the new
America calling your name, like a drug

Where are your choices?
What are your weapons?

And they lived hap . . .

Hail Mary

Like a lot of little girls growing up in the 1950s, I wanted to be a nun. Seriously.

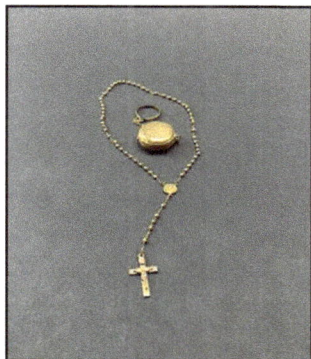

We were all overcome by the movie *The Song of Bernadette*, and Jennifer Jones became our first American Idol. We all wanted to be Bernadette, the impoverished little girl who was visited by the Virgin Mary in the grotto at Lourdes. She was so good . . . clear-eyed, beautiful, soft spoken, Oscar-winning Jennifer Jones.

So, I told my non-Italian grandmother about my decision one day and was a little surprised when she told me that it wasn't possible. I asked her why not. She broke the news to me that you had be Catholic to be a nun. I was crushed. It didn't seem fair.

I was a star in my Sunday School class, earning all the colored pictures of Jesus and the disciples by memorizing passages each week, and I won my little Bible (the one with my name burned in gold leaf on the cover) for answering the kind of trivia that was popular back then. (Not so much, "Why did God make you and all things?" as "Who got swallowed by the whale?" Catechism Lite.)

Anyway, I was shattered. I'd had my whole life planned: no muss, no fuss, no boys, no college – just walk into a church, prostrate myself in front of an altar, and somehow be transformed into a habited nun. Apparently, it was not so easy.

But other things confused me about this. Both my cousins had made their First Communions around age seven; our family was not invited. My best friend also had her "little bride of Christ" moment without me. When, at 15, I was to be confirmed into the Methodist Church, I wanted her there as moral support, but she had to get a letter from the Bishop giving her permission to attend. It came with instructions that she not take Communion if it was offered. Jesus would be mad at her if she did.

This made me squirm a little. What was this Catholic secret that I was not privy to? Only salvation and eternity were at stake! Was I not good enough to be a member of this club? Had my family done something wrong? Were we all going to hell?

Further complicating the issue was that I knew my father was a lapsed Catholic. As an Italian, he grew up in the faith, with all its attendant dos and don'ts and smells and obligations, a faith no doubt right out of the old country, back in ghettoized Brooklyn. And it was one that he felt comfortable abandoning. We never talked about this.

My great Aunt Anna (not by blood, just by friendship with my mother's mother) lived in a remarkable narrow Victorian row house in Woodhaven, Queens. I loved that house. It was just down the street from Forest Park, with its fantastic rolling hills and antique carousel. I would ride around and around and try to catch gold rings while I sat on the ornate gilded ponies or the giant painted rabbit and was transported for an afternoon into an unfamiliar and intriguing urban world.

The house had everything you would expect: tall ceilings, dark woodwork, pocket doors topped with leaded glass, black-and-white tiled bathrooms with high toilet tanks operated by pull chains. We sat in the large dining room, with its oversized mahogany furniture and paintings on three walls that simply scared the hell out of me.

One was a reproduction of a barely clad Saint Sebastian, shot full of arrows. The other was Bastien-Lepage's image of Joan of Arc, at the moment when the saints appear in her parents' garden, rousing her to fight against the English in the 100 Years War. Still another captured the moment when Lot's wife looked back and was turned into a pillar of salt.

As a child, I ate my offered sandwich – most often, the supremely non-Italian liederkranz cheese with raw onion on rye — surrounded by these profound images, just waiting for the floor to open up and swallow this little Protestant girl whole.

Unmarried Anna lived with her unmarried sister Barbara and their elderly guardian, who was simply known as "Auntie." Anna had lost her fiancée in World War I and never married. They attended the church down the street every single day. Anna and Barbara were retired from the telephone company and were original members of the prestigious Bell System Telephone Pioneers. Witty and straightlaced, they were the closest I would ever get to the hilarious spinster aunts from *Arsenic and Old Lace*, minus the homicide. But their Catholicism was what struck me, even as a little girl.

Their faith was undeniable. Anna wore a little silver and blue enamel charm of Mary (a "miraculous medal") on her watch band. Wooden and brass crucifixes hung over all the beds and there was iconography of all kinds around the house: kitschy paintings of the Sacred Heart of Jesus, the Virgin Mary in her flowing blue garment, Saint Francis with the birds, and Jesus knocking at the door. And once a year, Anna would take the train out to Massapequa to stay with us for a few days.

Sometimes Mom drove Anna to Hempstead, about 10 miles away, so she could meet an old childhood friend who had become a nun. We were ushered into a dark sitting room in a severe brick building to wait for her friend to come out, all wrapped up in miles of black robes with the classic white wimple, and she and Anna went off to a corner together. It was not lost on me that I was scared to death of her, the only nun that I had actually ever met. Anna usually brought her a little box of candy, for which she seemed very grateful, and they talked for a while, and then it was time to go. Anna stopped by and collected me and my mother and grandmother, and it always felt like some kind of secret pilgrimage.

If you were to come to my house in Massapequa, you might have noticed something a little out of place. I remember it well because I had to dust it every damned Saturday morning. On a shelf in the china cabinet was a small statue, mostly white, maybe six inches tall, of a religious figure. It had a stiff lace collar on its robe, wore a crown, and held a golden orb in one hand; the other hand was raised with the palm in a gesture of blessing. I learned years later that it was the Infant of Prague, and in our house, it always sat on top of a silver dollar coin.

I never knew where the heck it came from. The coin turns out to be an Irish tradition, to ensure that the household would never be hungry or in want. It must have been a gift to my grandmother from one Aunt Anna McCrorey . . .

As I write this, my Italian grandmother's rosaries are spread out in front of me. Somehow, I got them. In a family of Catholics, the Protestant kid gets the rosaries. Go figure. They are from Rome. I know this because the words "*Di Roma*" are stamped on the brass case and on the back of the crucifix. *Nonna* must have brought them over, and I have had them with me since the 1950s. And while I don't know how to use them myself, I know that my *nonna* must have put a lot of mileage on them: leaving home, crossing the ocean, marrying and having children, surviving the

Depression and whatever crushing loneliness you feel when you've left everything and everyone familiar behind.

Allora. I didn't get to be a nun, but as I run my fingers over the small round brass beads in her rosary, I can begin to imagine her struggles, her joys, her sacrifices, her faith. And that is enough for me.

I Think of My Grandmother on These Days

One hundred years ago, or more, she was
Sent on a ship to Mars, or so it must have seemed
All new, all promise, all apprehension, all so-not-this
To a country called New York, a new beginning

And now I am finally here, taking in her tastes
and smells
Her senses, her sea, hanging the laundry on a rack
In my tiny apartment, ninety miles from where
she lived
Ninety miles from where she left

A long-gone *nonna* and a once five-year-old girl
Under the same central Italy sky at last

Alive again, in time again
The way they never were before

La Famiglia

A few months after my
grandfather died in 1971,
my parents made a trip into
New York City to pick up
something they had left
there a few months before. I
was newly graduated from
college and home for the
summer, awaiting my
wedding that August, after
which I would move back
to Oneonta, New York so
my new husband could
finish his college degree. He was six years older than I
was but had only half-heartedly attended a local
college before we met.

When Mom and Dad came into the house with a
large bundle wrapped in brown paper, I was curious.
I did not know anything about this escapade. What
could it be?

We all walked over to the dining room table, and they
began to carefully unwrap it. The carved gold-leaf
frame was the first thing that I saw and then, little by
little, a black and white photo was revealed, surrounded
by a thick black velvet matting. It was beautiful. It was
la famiglia.

Turns out, while they were cleaning out my grandfather's house, they came across this old photo of the

family. Grandpa and Grandma Dini and their two sons, Ferdinando and Francesco. My uncle and father, aged maybe four and two, circa 1924. The photo was apparently in rough shape, so they had taken it to a restorer in the city to fix, enlarge, and frame. He had done a beautiful job.

Without hesitation, the framed photo was hung in a place of honor by the front door of our house in Massapequa — completely incongruous with the "Early American" furniture and brass starburst clock and sconces on the wall, left over from the '60s. When they moved to Palm Harbor, Florida eight years later, the photo went with them, and was hung in the dining room next to the hutch. And when my father died and we packed up the house, the photo came north with me and Tim, where it's had a place of honor in my office ever since.

I've always been a little curious about it. Almost every Italian American I know has a similar family photo taken in front of some classical backdrop, and I'll bet we all have pretty much the same questions: Where did they get the money to do this? Why did they do it? Was a copy sent back to their villages, to show that they were prospering in this new world? Were those clothes rented, or was this their big occasion best? Was this taken at said big occasion or did they go into a studio? Of course, I have no answers for any of this. It's just another family mystery that will never be solved.

My father is the little guy up on the pedestal. I love his little hands that seem to have too many fingers at first glance. But no, it's just the right number. And the bowl haircuts on him and my uncle are just adorable — which parent placed which ceramic bowl on their heads and clipped through howls and squirming, I wonder? Look at the little belted jackets with bows peeking out at the top, the short pants and leather ankle boots . . . it's all too precious.

My grandmother, always a large woman, looks gorgeous here. A gold bracelet and necklace (I imagine that, even in black and white), a small elegant purse dangling from her fingertips, perfectly coiffed hair (how on earth did they tame her curls?). And that dress! *Mamma mia!* A far cry from all those cotton flowered housedresses I remember.

My grandfather looks regal in his three-piece suit, and so proud of his family: a lovely wife, two healthy boys, work that could sustain them, and a future in America. It was what they came for. It was all they wanted.

Fast forward a few years, and the Depression hit. I'm sure times were hard, but my grandfather found work with the WPA to keep his family going. Before the end of the 1930s, the family moved out of Brooklyn and into the suburbs. Grandpa kept working for almost 40 more years, until throat cancer took him. He was one tough cookie. Never looked back.

He lived his Italian life at home in America, went to work with his Italian friends from the old neighborhood and saw his sons and their families grow a little less Italian every year. I don't know how he felt about that. A mixture of pride and regret, I suppose, that is never resolved in one generation.

Look at their eyes in this photo. Every one of them: Straight on, unwavering, beautiful, dark Italian eyes. Things will change after today. A crashed economy. Another world war. Death and more death. Unbearable pain. But also joy. Jobs. Weddings. Births. Gardens. Holidays. New beginnings.

Tutto andrá bene, la mia famiglia.

All will be well. All will be well.

PART TWO:

La figlia

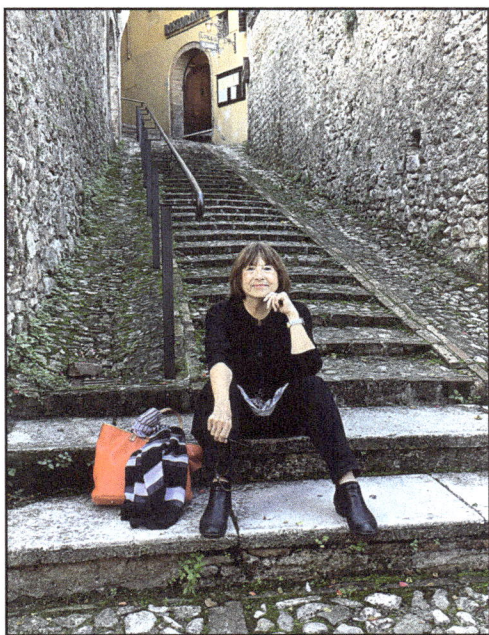

Your Blue-Eyed Boy

My mother's mother, Ida, stood about four foot eleven inches tall and wore a size three-and-a-half shoe. The entire time that I knew her (some 25 years) she wore variations of the classic "little old lady" shoe: chunky heeled, high vamp tie shoes that were distinguished as "everyday" (plain white, navy, or back leather) and "dressy" (black leather with a velveteen vamp and decorative little holes). For many years, we drove from our house in Massapequa into New York City to the Dr. Scholl's store on West 34th Street to buy shoes. Grandma would get her foot measured professionally (did they think it had grown since the last time?) and then view the new selections and pick out what she wanted. They had to be special ordered, of course, so a return trip was required to pick them up. All in all, this was a very expensive and time-consuming proposition for a very middle-class working family. But hey, Grandma needed shoes, right?

Progress came when Dr. Scholl opened a store in the suburbs. Hempstead was still a haul, but not the teeth-shattering, anxiety provoking trip that going into Manhattan was for my family. One year, maybe 1963 or 1964, when Mom and I were on the "return trip" to pick up what Grandma had ordered, we stopped for a few minutes at a bookstore. I was about 14 years old, already an experienced angst-ridden young poet, and was scouring the shelves for something suitably shocking to get my mother to buy for me (these were the days of $1.00 a week allowances, so I couldn't buy much for myself).

Anyway, Mom was getting impatient, standing in the front of the store and waiting for me to come out of the stacks. Then I found it: *100 Selected Poems*, by e.e. cummings. Originally published in 1923, this was the first Evergreen Edition, from 1959, and it bore a price tag of $1.75. I still have my copy, unglued front cover and all. I flipped through its pages and was very pleased with my choice. Here was a book that, by its very publication, told me that it was all right to break the rules. Lower case letters. Lines that stretched across and up and down the page. No discernable rhyme scheme. This would do nicely.

Of course, I had a passing acquaintance with cummings already, and had adopted his lower cases in some of my own poetry (as had most teen-aged girls at the time). But here (as was required in my household) was proof that this was legitimate. And that poetry itself could be lovely and nonsensical and horrifying — all at once.

I brought the book up to the cash register and my mother met me. She saw the little purple-covered book and rolled her eyes. But then something happened. The man behind the cash register looked at the book too, and then at me, and then back at the book. "You dig cummings, eh?" he said. My heart stopped. No one — not even my teachers, who knew I was an aspiring writer — had ever asked me what I "dug" before. I nodded feebly, trying to look as cool and grown-up as I possibly could, no mean feat for a chubby, introverted teenager whose idea of a good time was to actually get to listen to an entire side of the latest Peter, Paul, and Mary album in peace. "Let's see how much you know," he went on. I was doomed. Then my mother got interested, clearly enjoying this.

He opened the book and began reading, *Buffalo Bill's defunct* . . . and when he got to the line, . . . *and what I want to know is* . . . he stopped. Cold. And then he looked at me. And my mother glared at me. And for a split second the world came to an end. And then, out of nowhere known to me, came these words from my mouth: *how do you like your blue-eyed boy, Mister Death?*

The clerk smiled and handed me the book. My mother was gobsmacked. I said thank you to the man and walked out the door, ahead of my mother, trembling, but trying to remain calm. I had been tested by a total stranger and passed. I knew something. I had all I could do not to cry as I made my way out into the sunshine.

Years later, I still ask myself where the hell that line came from. Sure, I had heard the poem before, but I was not (and still am not) a memorizer. Somehow, that line of poetry stuck in my head, even at that early age. Even before I knew that I really would make my living among words. Even before I began to fill my room with books in earnest.

Songs from my Childhood

At Italian American weddings
And on my little blue Decca record player
Round and round they went
LPs, black and yellow and red
Oi, Mari . . . Torna a Surriento . . . Funiculi, Funicula . . .

Daddy singing *Eh, Cumpari*
Gli strumenti making me laugh:
A pling a pling, a toot a toot, and tipiti tipita tà

The 78s of Jimmy Durante
Umbriago … Young at Heart
Goodnight, Mrs. Calabash, wherever you are

Catch a Falling Star ... Arrivederci Roma
From the cardigan-ed Mr. C

*That's Amore . . . An Evening in Roma . . . Everybody
Loves Somebody . . .*
In that predictable Dean Martin smooth

Al Martino crooning
Al-Di-La . . . Mamma . . . Mala Femmina . . .

Fly Me to the Moon, Tony
And yes, I have gone from *Rags to Riches . . .*
Straight to the smiles of Lou Monte
*Lazy Mary . . . Bella Notte . . . Domenick the Christmas
Donkey*

I once saw the statue of Domenico Modugno
By the sea in Polignaro a Mare
As kids, we sang *Volare/Nel blu di pinto di blu*
Until we were hoarse
Never caring what the words meant
Except that we were flying

And then the other *blu*, Sinatra
Ol' Blue Eyes, Chairman of the Board
Who took us all down with that voice
With that pacing, with that hip, that cool
All the Way . . . September Song . . . A Very Good Year

All in my head, in my heart, still
Insistent as a *Mambo Italiano*

Anemic

I was always sick. My mother picked me up after school on Thursdays and we drove straight to the allergist. Turns out I was allergic to most growing things: grass, flowers, Christmas trees . . . cats . . .bees. . . dust and mold . . . and, the icing on the cake, penicillin.

On other days, it was the ear, nose, and throat doctor. My tonsils were removed twice and my adenoids, three times. Gym class threw me into coughing fits. I was weak. One of my family's quack doctors prescribed a (then) newfangled drug called cortisone to help clear up my respiratory ailments. That June when I got the shots, I was a skinny, lively, seven-year-old. When I went back to school in September, I was a sad, chubby, eight-year-old girl who didn't really know what the hell had happened to her. And who had just embarked on a lifelong battle with her weight.

I don't know if the cortisone was effective at all. But I do know that by the time I was 15 years old, I was so lethargic that my parents were worried. They took me to a doctor who pronounced me anemic and prescribed massive doses of iron supplements and regular B-vitamin shots. I took them for seven years, all the way through college — along with a special made-for-me dosage of gamma globulin that was painfully injected into my hips to boost my immune system. My pee smelled awful from the iron, and I wasn't getting any stronger.

In my mid twenties, my doctor told me to stop taking the iron supplements immediately. He had just read an article in a medical journal saying that it was completely ineffective against my kind of anemia and that it was probably damaging my liver. Question: *What kind of anemia doesn't respond to iron and B vitamins?* Answer: *Thalassemia. Mediterranean anemia. Common among people from that part of the world: Greeks and Italians, mostly.*

My father was tested. He had it, too. Nothing to do. We had thalassemia minor. Stop the iron. Eat more leafy greens. Live with it. When you're tired, rest.

I was warned not to marry another Italian because, if he also had a minor strain, we could pass along one of the killer major strains to our children. At that point, I was engaged to an Italian American.

Fortunately, no children came of the union and the marriage was over within ten years. But it was during that period, as I look back on it now, that I first started paying attention to the fact that I had real Italian roots. That I was made up of Italian genes, just like my dark-haired, dark-eyed *cugini*.

In being marked, in some way, by this disorder, I realized that I belonged to a tribe. I wasn't just this half-breed; my ethnicity had chosen me. Ridiculous.

But it was a start . . .

Daddy Toast

Grandpa's aluminum toaster was a death trap:

The grey cloth power cord frayed,
The tiny cardboard protector piece spilling
Out of the plug bottom, prongs all askew

The ornate sides still standing stately
Until you tried to move them
To put the bread inside

A disaster, pure and simple
A pretty relic, that is all
Eventually deemed unsafe and impractical

With no modern toaster, Dad improvised
Toast on a long fork, over the open flame
Of our gas range

First one side, then the other
Trying not to burn it, using the
Age-old toasted marshmallow technique

My sandwiches were blackened
But I didn't care
Daddy toast was good, was ours

Something we did together, while Mom
Used the newfangled toaster oven which
Neither of us could comprehend

In Sulmona, Daddy toast is what we have
Is what we look forward to in the morning
A little charred history with our *fichi marmellata*

Nino

I worked in the advertising business in New York
City in the 1970s and into the '80s. I started out as a
secretary in a firm with a very good reputation for
its training and research-based approach to creating
advertising. We managed some of the largest, most
prestigious accounts in the world at the time: Hath-
away, Rolls Royce, Guinness, Merrill Lynch, American Express. If there was an equivalent in advertising
to the "white shoe" law firm, we were it.

Ethnicity was the kiss of death in our agency world.
But there was Joe, the mailman, who came from Malta
and Jack, the repro guy, who was Armenian, and you'd
better get along with both of them if you wanted your
work life to run smoothly. And then there were a few
of us secretaries: on my floor, there was a Jew, a Central
European, and me.

My astonishing rise to lower middle management
reads like *Rosemary's Baby*. The staff assistant for the
group I supported had a horrible automobile accident.
She would be out for months, with a broken body
and a wired jaw. I meekly went into my bosses' office
and asked if I could take over her work. They were a
little skeptical but agreed, because report season was
coming up and they were desperate.

Bottom line? I did just fine, and earned two more promotions while I was there, but very little additional
money. In 1980, I was out for a week with a quadfecta
of wisdom tooth extractions. I was miserable. I had

been overworked and underpaid and life pretty much sucked at that moment. I had been asking for an assistant for months, but nothing ever came of it.

When I returned to work, I found that an assistant had been hired for me. Not the best way to get one — I would have liked to have been involved in the hiring process — but I was hopeful that things were about to get better for me. Turns out, he was a Harvard MBA with not one day of work experience. He would not take instruction from me and told me that he was hired for his marketing expertise and not to write some stupid competitive reports for the client.

I reminded him that he had absolutely no marketing expertise, and then checked his personnel file (remember personnel files?) before I talked to my boss. To my surprise, I learned that he was hired at a starting salary that was $10,000 more than I was making after eight years.

For a few years, my client was Pepperidge Farm, a division of the Campbell Soup Company. One presentation season, I had to give part of the presentation to the client. My first one ever. I was scared to death, but I walked into the dark conference room that morning, went up to the overhead projector (remember overhead projectors?) and started. Later that afternoon, after the client had gone, my boss came in to critique me. He said I did okay, but that I should learn to sit on my hands when I presented. What are you, he asked. Italian or something?

The talk with my boss did not go well. He would not give me a raise and made it very clear that I was stuck in this situation, with no way out. Fortunately, I had brought my own way out to the meeting — a letter of resignation, effective immediately. I never looked back.

So, you ask, *Who's Nino?*

One of my promotions had taken me to work for another Italian American — to my knowledge, the only one in a management position in the agency at that time. He was a man adept at writing and presentations and at making people feel like they were being listened to. He was not named Nino.

He was charged one year with planning the big client year-end dinner. All the bosses would be there from both the client side and the agency side. It was a huge deal. He and I worked on this project together, considering venues and menus and were excited to try and do something a little different, something our New York City-loathing clients would enjoy. But shortly before the event was finalized, his boss' boss called him into the office.

It seems that arrangements had already been made in one of the poshest restaurants in the city. Lutece or The Quilted Giraffe . . . I can't remember now . . . some place that, in cost and snob appeal, was anathema to our client. When my boss asked why the project had been pulled from him, he got this answer: *Why, where would you have taken us, Nino? The Hong Kong Inn?*

I learned a lot of lessons from that experience: That no matter how far up in the organization Italian Americans went, we were still considered inferior. We were not to be trusted. We had questionable taste. We were worthy of ridicule. We had to go along to get along. And the only recourse was to leave, at great cost to our self-esteem, career path and, usually, bank account.

"Nino" stayed, then left, then went back. I freelanced for most of the rest of my professional life. It had its ups and downs, and it surely came with a cost. But I knew that it was the best way to ensure that I would never be in that position again.

Holding Up Our Half of the Sky at the End of the Twentieth Century

Electricity worries me.
So does Aviation.
Physics eluded me all through school.
Math nightmares follow me into my forties.
Waiting for a meeting to begin, I look out the window
of this polite conference room, and cannot believe
what I see . . . across the street, in a big building,
sitting at a major intersection, someone has hung
a life preserver on the window of their office.

I imagine it is a woman's office.
I imagine that another woman might also be worried,
fiddling with damp switches,
flying old planes to unsafe places,
opening doors, windows — lifting — with the
wrong resistance,
doing the longhand when the batteries go dead.

I imagine that another woman coping, thriving
on these things,
holding up her half of the sky at the end of the
twentieth century,
would still want to turn, at the end of the day,
and know
there was the possibility of rescue.

Intern

There were two of us that summer
But the married engineer named Frank
—The one with the big mouth—
Said I had some sex appeal
And the other one was nothing but a cold fish

Late '60s and I was working in a defense plant
Courtesy of my father

The group sat close under the buzzing fluorescents
Side-by-side in three rows of Steelcase desks
My unsure hands directing my useless fingers
To thump the keys on a mocha brown IBM Selectric
Where every day I watched the ball turn and wondered
How the hell it always knew which letter to stop at

It made so much noise, rattling on its metal typing stand
That everybody knew when I got stuck, made a mistake
Or simply got too tired to go on

NavSpecs is what they were — the incessant
filing and updating
Of the minute changes in the specifications of war:
This plane, that coupling, a new engine, a better bolt
Old one out New one in Punch Open Close Discard
Repeat
Repeat
Repeat

Every day, lunch was three oatmeal cookies stacked
In noisy cellophane, eaten in the bathroom stall,
a juice
Snagged from the cafeteria on the way back
to my desk

Don't talk to me
Don't look at me
I will work and no more

The big black and white clock on the wall slammed
Get me out
Get me out
Get me out

The First Time I Saw Italy

I didn't want to go. Italy was never on my bucket list.

I grew up with a father who never wanted to go, a grandfather who never went back, and friends of my grandfather's who did go back and returned with horror stories about being financially drained by their relatives. So I decided that Italy was not a place I wanted to go. *If you're American, they think you're rich*, Rosario said. *All they want is your money*, Enrico said.

Also, there was never any mention of actual family back in Italy, so I never knew if I had anyone to visit. Did my *nonno* have brothers and sisters? Did my *nonna* have a family there? No one talked about it. In fact, there was some confusion about where my grandparents were even from.

I traveled to England, Wales, Canada, France, Belgium, and Bermuda long before I saw Italy. It came about because (1) Tim decided it was high time I put aside my prejudices about Italy, and (2) some friends from church were organizing a trip and asked us to be part of the group. It is an understatement to say that the decision to go changed my life.

In the fall of 1999, our friend Tom called and asked if we would like to be included in the planning stages of a possible trip to Tuscany. He said he had gotten information about villas from an agency and wanted to put together a small group to talk about it. We said yes, and soon found ourselves part of a group of eight people who would travel the following June and launch ourselves into an adventure in the little village of Cistio, northeast of Florence, in the lovely (unknown to us) territory of the Mugello.

And so it was that Tom and John, Jack and Patrick, Sandi and Katie, and Tim and I set off in two ridiculous Fiat Multipla SUVs in the days before cell phones and headed for parts unknown. We went to Florence several times, the first time getting stuck in the parking lot elevator for 20 minutes with a bunch of rowdy locals. It was as panic-inducing as it sounds.

We went to Lucca and walked around on the famous city wall. We went to Pisa for the *Luminaria di San Ranieri* on Sandi's birthday. We ordered a gorgeous whipped cream cake from the local *pasticceria* on John's birthday, and I learned the word *auguri* for the first time.

Patrick recited Shakespeare for us at the *Teatro Romano* in Fiesole. We met scorpions and snails. We gasped at the monstrous Benetti yachts in the harbor in Viareggio. We saw rain so hard we thought our villa — a 9th century converted grain mill — would be washed down the precarious mountain on which it was perched. We fell in love with the wine, with the olive trees, and with the fresh air and sense of freedom that we experienced there. And I wrote.

Italy was the first place that truly inspired me as a writer. Before that, it was all assignments. Here was the stuff of family, of tradition, of fear, of desire . . . here was a culture I could sink my teeth into and that, in some ways, I felt I already knew a little about.

And I thought, sadly, about how bad it must have been for my grandparents — and thousands like them — to leave this countryside for the complete unknown. To risk everything. To lose everything. To start anew. The ocean crossing alone would have scared me to death.

During those two weeks, we bonded as a group of friends and we bonded as travelers. Group travel doesn't always work out (as anyone who's tried it can confirm) but this trip worked. We ate breakfasts at home, had lunches out, and dinners were often just heavy *antipasti* in the garden. Cheese, salami, and crusty bread . . . wine, friends, stories, and warm Tuscan breezes filled with the scent of jasmine and freshly mowed grass. Pure magic.

We explored the museums and churches of Florence and John, our personal historian, told us which were the can't-miss sites. Being face-to-face (so to speak) with Michelangelo's *David* and then Donatello's *David* (which, by the way, I prefer) . . . seeing Botticelli's *Birth of Venus* and Ghiberti's *Gates of Paradise* was more extraordinary in every way than I had imagined.

We drove around a lot, stopping at wineries, climbing up to the top of Brunelleschi's dome and the towers in San Gimignano for breathtaking views. We strolled through the small city of Borgo San Lorenzo near our villa and were welcomed into a corner table at a local restaurant, Ristorante Gli Artisti, for one of the best meals of our lives. We let it happen, and there was no going back.

Since this trip, over 20 years ago, I have returned to Italy many times. I have traveled to Sicily, to Milan, to Verona, Vicenza and Venice, to Rome and Florence, to the Ligurian Coast, the Cinque Terre, to Como and Ferrara, and to the breadbasket cities of Modena, Mantua, and Parma. I have seen the Ferrari Museum and eaten great food in Bologna. I have travelled to Assisi, Perugia, Deruta, and Gubbio. I have been awed by the Byzantine mosaics in Ravenna and by the quiet beauty of Ravello and the Amalfi Coast in the off-season. I have embraced the wild beauty of Le Marche and could easily call Rafael's city of Urbino home. I had been gobsmacked by Matera, charmed by Trani, and fallen in love with Lecce.

And then I discovered Abruzzo, the gateway to Cuomo's *mezzogiorno*. Southern Italy. I had come home to a place I had never been, nor had any roots in. Is it even possible?

It is a little ironic that my first trip to Italy was centered on Tuscany; we even spent a day in Siena, but couldn't find a restaurant that was open, so we moved on after taking in the Piazza del Campo — where the famous *palio* is held every summer — and then gaping at the huge fresco of "The Allegory of Good and Bad Government" in the city hall. I was so close to my *nonno's* birthplace and had no idea.

Timmy Takes Us on a Road We Should Not Travel But, as Usual, It All Works Out

We could only go so far
down this rutted dry dirt road

But it was in his favorite valley:
The one where Raino and Corfinio take you
Up to Vittorito, the one near the abandoned
Farmhouse he has his eye on

There is a river, which he wanted to put his feet in
Despite the May chill, a sacred river
But we could never get close enough in spite of trying

We parked in the road by recently plowed fields
With bamboo tepees arranged to support
Whatever had been planted: trees with white flowers
Lined the narrow road; sambucco, we've been told

The rented car got stuck and muddy
Thanks to rain the night before
Still, the sun shone on us and on the mountains
Melting the snow that remains in late May

The spiny artichokes were coming up fast
The vines were starting to flaunt their tiny fruit
The horses had foaled
The cows had calved
The pigs had piggled
And life was starting up again

I did not know how white the clouds could be against
a clear blue sky
I did not know there were so many shimmering
shades of green
I did not know how sharp a sudden breeze could be
I did not know my heart could hold so much joy

Gabriele, the Dog, and the Genius

Gabriele and his blonde spotted dog, 16 years old and nearly deaf and blind, walk slowly together in *sestiere* San Marco, looking curiously like brothers. Gabriele's sandy grey ponytail and the dog's floppy sandy ears move in time to the water in the canals being stirred by the pivoting gondolas in front of Venice's Hard Rock Café. The staff at our hotel know Gabriele and his dog. They approve of our encounter when we tell them the story later.

The two go to work at the small art store every day. The dog takes up his post on a raised canvas bed behind the cash register. He is even too old to greet the customers any more. He just sleeps, shifting every now and again to catch a sea bird in his dreams.

Gabriele, meanwhile, gets the shop ready for the tourists — too many tourists, he says. They buy a postcard or two or a cheap print of the Rialto Bridge and leave. But they are not his market, anyway. No, Gabriele is here for the artists of Venice. He sells what they most need: canvas, brushes, paints, mats, drawing pencils, and fine Venetian papers to line the covers of hand-made books. The tourists see none of this.

We speak to Gabriele and ask about an artist whose work we have just seen on the island of Torcello the previous day. His name is Leonardo D'Este. Gabriele's eyes widen as we say the name. Yes, he says, he is a friend. A most gifted artist. A customer, too, he says — he was just here yesterday buying supplies. He says

"Leonardo" and puts out one hand, palm up. Then he says "Leonardo" again and puts out the other hand. It is a comparison. The two Leonardos. We all agree.

Young Leonard (age 44 at the time) is a master portraitist. We tell Gabriele the story of how we met his mother, Aurora, on Burano, at the restaurant where he works as a waiter. He was not there, but another waiter called Aurora and told her that some people had come to speak to Leonardo. He was back in Venice, buying supplies, it seems. We told Gabriele about how she is so proud of her son that she took is to his studio to see his work, apologizing as we walked for the humbleness of what we were about to see and the fact that nearby construction was making a lot of dust.

He paints in the morning when the light is good, and then works at the restaurant when he is finished. He does only commissions, it turns out, and only from life. Never from photographs. Twenty sittings per portrait. When we saw his work at the restaurant (Villa 600 on Torcello) we thought we were looking at old masterworks. Rembrandt, perhaps, or John Singer Sargent. But on careful study, it is clear that he has contemporized their style a bit, while maintaining the old light emerging miraculously from the dark background. The faces are fantastic. Genius.

Leonardo's small studio is strewn with books by both Rembrandt and Sargent. He is self-taught, and he studies them. His latest commission is enormous — an El Greco-sized full body portrait of a man with a background of glorious red and gold fabric. The portrait takes up most of the studio. Aurora shows us where the subject stands, where Leonardo stands, how he runs up to get close and copy the details, then runs back for a full view. We saw some completed works, one better than the next. His models are often family members or humble workers from the restaurant whom he transforms with furs, pearls, and fine feathered caps. He even had a small unfinished self-portrait which helped fill in some of the blanks about who Leonardo is. His is an interesting face: narrow, imperfect, not beautiful, but full of character. And maybe a little sadness, or maybe we are bringing that.

The studio is very small, devoid of any kind of technology save electric lights. This drives his mother mad. No *telefonino*, she laments. Perhaps he is missing another commission and she cannot reach him. *I will kill him; no, really, I will kill him,* she says in her Venetian dialect which, astonishingly, we sort of understand.

We leave our information with Aurora and tell her we'd like to contact Leonardo for a self-portrait. This shocks her, and we have to say it several times: auto ritratto. We want a portrait of her son, the son we have never met? Yes. He is a master and we want his self-portrait while it is still affordable. I think she is not sure of us, but agrees to tell him when he returns.

Next day we meet Gabriele and his dog. It seems that while we were talking to Aurora, Leonardo was here with Gabriele, buying more paint. Incredible. The dog shifts gently in his bed. Perhaps there is a little smile.

I'll Make a Little Snack

These days, I am the part-time executive director of a small non-profit in Salem, Massachusetts. To introduce more people into the historic home, I open it to some local organizations for their meetings. At one such early morning event several years ago, I ushered the ladies into the mid-19th century dining room, where they would hold their first meeting.

They looked at the table and one of them said, meekly, "You don't have to feed us." She had noticed the pitcher of juice and the little scones I'd placed on a plate for them, along with cups and napkins. I said, "Nobody comes to my house without being fed."

It had never occurred to me to not have something for them. This was a group of private citizens, volunteers, who were doing fantastic outreach to underserved populations in the region. How could I invite them into my home at 9:00 in the morning and not have some breakfast for them? It was just a little snack. The tradition continues, nearly ten years later, and now they seem at ease with my small offerings.

There was a telling photo on Facebook a while back. It showed a table about 20 feet long, laden with trays of salami, cheese, lasagna, cookies, pasta, bread, sausages, sandwiches, and so on, reaching as far out of the frame as you could see, with an aproned-clad *nonna* sitting down at the end. The caption read, "Italians be like, 'We'll put out a few snacks.'"

Che cosa?!? It was like this at my house. If we were expecting six people, Daddy cooked for 12 because you never knew who might show up. There was always a coffee cake in the kitchen in case company dropped by. There were always choices. If you wanted a cookie, you could have an Oreo, a Lorna Doone, a Ginger Snap, or a Golden Raisin Biscuit. Appetizer? There were Swedish Meatballs, Pigs in Blankets, Shrimp Cocktail, or Roasted Peppers in olive oil. And always two entrees. Turkey and lasagna . . . Roast beef and veal parmesan . . . Honey Ham and spaghetti and meatballs.

There was a food generosity even in the least well-off Italian-American homes. Food meant love, it meant nurturing, it meant attention and creativity and even competition (among the cooks) and it forced everybody to sit at the table together and be a family for a while. I see this same thing expressed in the Italian families at whose homes I dine. And if you've ever had a Sunday lunch at a restaurant in Italy, you know not to schedule anything else for the day. It is a three-to-four-hour affair with several generations sitting around talking, joking, shouting at the kids to be quiet, and laughing it up with the chef/owner, who is probably a cousin.

A while back, another Italian American friend and I hosted an evening at which we introduced our friends to our beloved Abruzzo. We both agreed to bring "a few snacks" and the table looked pretty much like the one I described earlier. We laughed. There are no half measures when it comes to Italians feeding people.

Our friends were treated to a remarkable evening of Italian food, wine, and stories, and both hostesses ate well for the next week, even after a group of 30 had plowed through the table like vultures.

I remember my *nonna* and my father's cousins in the kitchen on special Sundays at his *comare's* house, all cooking together. It was a competitive sport. Their uniform was the flowered apron and a *mapinni* — a dishtowel jauntily flung over one shoulder — and the object of the game was to kill us all with food. And then came the *caffe coretto* — *espresso* with Sambuca or whiskey — and we could relax.

Order an early evening drink in Italy, and it will probably come with enough snacks to constitute dinner. Go to an Italian home and you'll be crushed under the weight of the courses. Accept an invitation from your Italian American friend and expect a multi-layered feast. That's just the way it is.

Stati zitto e mangia! (Shut up and eat!)

I Pomodori:
Even the Dirt Dreams of Italy

My father showed me what to do
In the straight planted fields of summer
Long green sweet peppers growing alongside
Baseball-sized red tomatoes, bright,
Staked and tied against the wind
Their rich leaves gluttoning the sun, the
Fruit exhaling the promised flavors
That tempted us for weeks

When I lived in New York City
I grew small tomatoes, potted, on the seventh floor
Terrace of a brownstone on East 68th Street
My boyfriend called them M30s
After the crosstown bus fumes from below
That came to rest, probably, eventually,
On the heroic crop, thriving in the soil against all odds

I didn't care: one tiny bite, the seeds
And juices cascading down my fingers
Or popped into my mouth, whole and sweet,
Brought Daddy back to those suburban summer fields,
And with him, a place I did not yet know I would
Come to crave

Crucified

When I was a kid in Massapequa, I hung out mainly
with three friends: Barbara, Barbara, and Rhonnie.
Two of them were Jewish, but one of the Barbaras
was a half-breed like me, only with an Italian mother,
instead of an Italian father. We used to joke that you
almost never saw my father and her mother together
in the same room: they were so much alike, we suspected they might be the same person. Just this year
we learned that they grew up just one block apart in
Sunset Park, Brooklyn.

We would hang out at each other's houses after school
and on weekends, but I was at her place more than
she was at mine. My mother once asked me why, and
I said something about there being more noise in her
house and that I liked that. The noise at Barbara's
house came mostly from her Neapolitan mother.

Except for the show albums I would play on my
mother's console record player, my house was as quiet
as a morgue. Seldom were voices raised and then,
only behind closed doors. If I was deemed unruly,
I would get sent to my room (not a big punishment
for an introvert); once or twice I got the back end of a
hairbrush. Of course, I was a perfect child, so I can't
imagine why.

Barbara's house was another matter entirely. She
was the oldest of three kids; I was an only child. The

presence of two other beings vying for their mother's attention was something new to me and I watched their interactions like I would watch a documentary. There was the jockeying for position, the false accusations, the petty betrayals . . . it was all there. I loved it. Cries of "He started it!" and "She touched me!" filled the room. Barbara's mother bubbled over with stress and emotion — you could see it in her body language — and finally, she would break.

She was usually in the kitchen when this happened, stirring a big pot of sauce or doing something to get ready for the evening meal before she had to run out to her second job. She would turn around, wipe her hands on her apron, and brandish a wooden spoon in the direction of the offending child. Then it came, loud and clear:

"If you don't shut up, I'm going to crucify you!"

The first time she said this in front of me, I was utterly and completely horrified. I had never heard anything like it. My exposure to crucifixion came from those horrible scenes in *The Greatest Story Ever Told*. It was a bloody, gruesome, headache-inducing, pain-in-the-gut kind of scene that we Protestants hardly ever talked about. Our crucifixes are empty; Catholic crucifixes have Himself hanging from the cross. To me, it was an unthinkable thing to say to a child.

But it ran off Barbara and her sibs like water down a duck's back. The kids had been waiting for it. They giggled, then stopped, and usually dispersed. They had achieved their goal of making mommy explode.

Ultimately, nobody was ever crucified, no blood was shed, and life went on. But when Barbara's mother became my Girl Scout leader, along with my mother, I minded my ps and qs, let me tell you. She just might have had a hammer and nails in that huge green purse of hers . . .

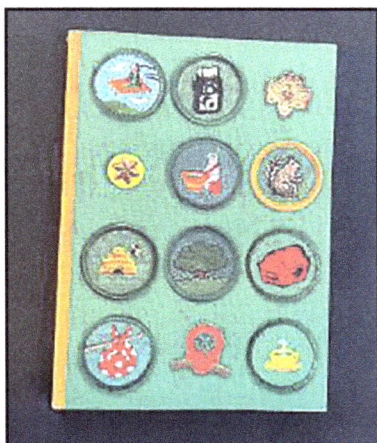

Holy Day, Levittown

A chubby fourteen-year-old takes a ride
with her father
to visit his godmother one Easter Sunday.

Women in the kitchen, doing dishes, noisy,
punctuating space
with hands, with pouts, with pitch, talking
women things.

Men in the cement block basement, now cooled
and almost dark —
the big table dismantled — toddlers playing
in the corner, a low ceiling
cramping the height of no tall Italian.

Bored by the women jabbering nonsense,
half-English-half-Italian, fabricated dialects,
ridiculous giggles,
she opts for the basement, enduring teases,
growth spurt jokes,
crude snickers from young uncles holding
dainty cups of mud and anisette,
hard at work at Sunday target practice in their
opened shirts and tight black pants.

They shoot a .22 at a paper target on the
concrete wall; the ricocheting
shells, too hot to touch "ping" when they hit the floor.

Sweet liquor.
And the babies.
And the gun.
A casual trinity on such a day.

Empty sounds of the womenfolk
wafting down the stairs.

Only Child

On my block, Surrey Lane, there were only two houses with only children: ours and Regina Sullivan's. The other houses — all small capes consisting of three bedrooms and two baths — were bursting with large Catholic families. If memory serves, the Collins house had six children, the Cronins had five, the Cirellas had four and, down the block, the Pfeffers had eight. There was even a family across the street that fostered five girls. I felt like a freak.

No one to play with, no one to learn how to fight with, no sibling rivalries to act out, no ally in the war against the parents, and no one to help with the mysteries of the opposite sex.

For much of the time, I was alone.

I was an introverted kid. In Fourth Grade, my teacher sent me home with a note telling my parents that she was worried about me. "She even asks permission to sharpen her pencil," was one of the things my mother told me she had written. I thought I was supposed to. I was raised to be polite, to not speak unless spoken to, to not be too forthcoming with any thoughts of my own.

Turns out that, in addition to being raised shy and polite, I also experienced a severe hearing loss about this time brought about by impacted sinuses. So my teacher's ultimate suggestion that I be placed in the "slow" track was roundly ignored. Score one for the parents.

But I soon found a new way to survive. I read. I listened to music constantly. And I wrote. At the age of eight, I experienced the first outside affirmation for my work: a four-line ditty about the horrors (to a Myers-Briggs INFJ) of April Fool's Day was included in the school district literary magazine. I was thrilled. I knew what I wanted to do with my life.

Our across-the-street neighbor, Mrs. Cirella, gave my mother a gift one summer day when I was about 12. It was a Lladro-like statue of a young kerchiefed girl, head down, reading a book that she held in her lap. She said it reminded her of Lindy (which is what the neighbors called me). I used to sit on the front stoop of our house with either my nose in a book or, pencil in hand, in a journal of some kind.

Which made socialization that much harder. I spent a lot of time up in my room, too, reading and writing. Let me take a moment now to express my deep thanks to my teacher — fiery, red-headed, dramatic Ruth Rafkin — for her enthusiastic encouragement and a distinct boho style which I have taken with me, even after all these years.

I still have many of the journals I wrote from the time I was about 15 and took my first elective English class: one semester of journalism and one semester of creative writing. And somewhere in a box I also have the stories that we had to write in Fifth Grade, neatly bound in hand-made folios, secured with those brass plated round-head fasteners. I rediscover these each time we make a move — along with some pretty serious high school history papers on the Holocaust and Mario Savio and the Free Speech Movement at UC Berkeley. Wasn't I a fun kid?

The point is, I would stay up in my room a lot. My mother would often call from downstairs, "What are you doing, Linda?" to which my standard reply was, "I promise, Mom, I'm not having any fun." She seemed somehow relieved by that.

The truth was, I *was* having fun. I read voraciously. I read everything I was supposed to read for school, and then all the extra credit books, too. I was mesmerized by myth: Greek and Roman mythology and the Norse eddas. I had my own well-worn copy of *Bulfinch's Mythology.*

I eschewed the usual girl stuff — *Little Women, Jane Eyre, Wuthering Heights* — and instead read John Hersey and Ernest Hemingway. I shivered with glee at *An Occurrence at Owl Creek Bridge* by Ambrose Bierce. A big fan of Washington Irving and Edgar Allen Poe, I also devoured tales of the paranormal.

I felt particularly close to John Gunther's *Death Be Not Proud*, about his 17-year-old son who bravely faced death from a brain tumor. I felt a dramatic early death coming on, too, and sometimes went to sleep counting the people who would be sorry that they were so mean to me before I died.

When I was 13 years old, I entered another writing contest. Sponsored by the library system, it was for an essay about reading. I won one of the prizes and my award was to choose any book I wanted from among the library shelves. My choice was easy: *To Kill a Mockingbird*, one of the recently published books I'd read about in *The New York Times*. The librarians were concerned, but once again my parents — who had no idea what the book was about — sided with me, and my wish was granted.

So now I learned that fame is fun, that some writing is dangerous, and that maybe I had a flair for this. I continued to write throughout high school and college, contributing to the literary magazines and to the political magazine at college. I graduated with a degree in Liberal Arts English and promised my father that I'd get a master's degree in Secondary Education, but I only lasted six days in my student teaching assignment. I was hopeless. I knew nothing about dealing with kids. I stopped, left school — nine credits shy of that degree — and got a job at the local department store, selling loose candy and greeting cards.

By this time, my father was worried. Both my girl cousins had gone on to teaching careers. Since he grew up at a time when women got married (first prize) or had mostly temporary careers in nursing or teaching ("something to fall back on"), he had no idea what was to become of me. Neither, really, did I.

I could type pretty well and signed up at a few employment agencies when I finally left my upstate

New York college town and moved to New York City in 1973. I got a job as a secretary, first in the publishing business, and then in the advertising business, where I worked like a dog for years trying to please the unpleasable and advance in a career that was never really open to me.

All this time later, I can chalk up my corporate failure largely to that well of doubt that bubbles up every so often. That fraud feeling. That total lack of confidence combined with being a solo act and having a misguided desire to please everybody. I didn't know what my options were. I didn't even know what I didn't know. Sounded too much like Daddy in the defense plant. I got tired of it and left.

Did I have to be Italian to experience this? Of course not. But I think being the child of a gun-shy first-generation Italian made it hard for me to gain traction. My parents were always there to pull me back from asserting myself, from taking risks, from moving outside their comfort zones. Except for writing, which — I think — they thought was kinda cute and didn't take very seriously.

I remember one December in the 1980s when I invited my parents to come into New York City for the day. I wanted to take them around to see the spectacular decorated windows and, walking up Fifth Avenue, we came to Tiffany & Co. I started through the revolving door, with my mother right behind me. When we got inside, we noticed Dad still out on the sidewalk. We went back around through the revolving door and I asked him if he was coming in. I'll never forget what he said to me: *No. And you shouldn't either. We don't belong here.*

I thought about what he said for a second or two, and it took every ounce of courage I had to turn around and re-enter the revolving door. Mom came, too. It broke my heart that Dad stayed outside in the cold, but he did. Even into his sixties, he felt there were places he did not belong, places that would see him as unworthy, places that would look down their noses at him. Had I gotten too big for my britches during my time in New York? He certainly thought so, but I would not be pulled back this time.

It was a kind of beginning for me, but I could not have predicted what would happen next.

I Tried to be the Perfect Daughter, But My Daddy Died Anyway

That is a sentence that I have written before, but which has gone nowhere. I even tried the concept once in poetry:

To my Father in Fiji, 1942

In this photo, you are twenty
The smallest in your unit by far
Maybe the only Italian
Wavy black hair and an eager smile
Odd for someone so young and in such a place
You are ready for anything
Tailored and wiry like a terrier

You waited 50 years to tell me about this mission,
About your work out there in the South Pacific
As a child, I always imagined warm breezes and
wacky sailors

Star-crossed lovers never letting each other go;
Flying overhead, keeping the islands Safe
for Democracy
Or, if not that, for an endangered way of life

Instead, I find out how the government got you
from New York
To San Francisco to Hawaii, not yet a state, and
how you had
To hitchhike from there to Australia on your own

No protection, no cover, just get there son, and
if you make it
We'll tell you what to do next

I want to write about the madness of those Open Orders
I want to write about how you were an aerial gunner
Hanging off the belly of the plane
I want to write about how dangerous your
missions were

How the very reason I have these pictures is because
You were gunning for a unit that did recon
photography missions
Going out to map the place by plane so
Uncle Sam would know
Exactly where to drop the bombs

I want to write about the islanders in the pictures
Before they fade away completely
But you've told me so little, and the notes on the back
That you wrote to my mother provide very few clues

You told me you trapped fish in holes in the coral reefs
And ate coconut and chickens
You said the islanders were kind to you
You said that when you went to Australia for R&R
You got ration books that you traded for socks
and razors
And that the MPs bought you whisky

I want to grab all you
Beautiful young men by the shoulders and say
Thank You/Damn You/What the hell made you go on?

• • •

That's as far as I have ever gotten. There was never an answer to my "What did you do in the war, Daddy?" question. My father never talked about it. Not until I was about 50 years old and he and I were sitting together on his back porch in Florida years after my mother was gone. He said he needed to tell me something. It was about the war. It was about what he did.

He opened an odd metal box holding a bunch of photographs. His was a reconnaissance unit, he said. I saw photos of dozens of black and white military photos hung up on a clothesline inside a dark building. They were plotting the movements of the Japanese. It was dangerous work. He was an aerial gunner. Something had happened. And then he gave me the metal box and the photos – a box that he had made in the Navy. Hard rivets, like on an airplane, made from airplane scraps. Everybody in his unit had made one.

I never found out anything more. I don't know if he ever killed anybody, but I doubt that you can be an aerial gunner and not kill somebody. I only know that he survived and that he came home. He came home with a tropical infection that almost cost him an arm, and an ulcer that cost him much of his stomach. Still, he held it all in. Daddy was like that.

The important things stayed stuffed, while the little things caused explosions.

Daddy died in January 2001, about two weeks after Tim and I had visited him in a nursing home in Florida. We lied and said he was in rehab. It was partly true, because he'd fallen and hurt his arm, so he was in rehab for his trauma, but he wasn't getting out of there. He was grumpy and he was hallucinating.

I've since learned that Parkinson's Disease can cause that; he had been diagnosed with Parkinson's but didn't believe it because he showed almost no sign of tremors. One morning, from his hospital bed, he

called out his brother's name: Fred. More than once.
Fred had predeceased him by a few years. Fred was in
the room there with him. His big brother had come to
accompany dad on his last mission. I loved that, and I
wept. He was gone just two weeks later.

Becoming Italian

That afternoon on the porch explained a lot, and very little, at the same time. I did not really know what to make of the arc of my father's life. And I saw so many similarities to my own up until that time that it made me a little uncomfortable. Feeling an impostor, not fitting in, deferring, deferring, deferring . . . but finally coming back to family.

On more than one occasion, Tim has asked me why I consider myself Italian when I am really only half Italian. When he researched the Raynor side of the family and determined that I was probably related to the Viking chief Ragnar, I sort of shrugged. I did not care. *But your mother's family has been here for almost 400 years,* he'd say, and I'd think, *So what?*

During my childhood and adolescence, life with my mother was a little odd and not what anybody would consider nurturing. I think she always believed we were in competition for my father's affections and she belittled me whenever an opportunity arose.

When I was home from college one Christmas, we went out shopping. I saw a beautiful dress in Orbach's that nearly broke my heart. I still remember it: black velvet top with a full red plaid taffeta skirt and, when she saw me looking at it, she said matter-of-factly, *You don't need that. Nobody asks you out.* A history of hurtful behavior made me bit by bit disengage from any identity with my mother's side of the family.

There is no doubt that I am my father's daughter and I have more or less forgiven him his fears, his insecurities, and his hurtful behavior subsequent to my mother's death.

Take that confirmation celebration I wrote about. Turns out my father, I learned many years later, was so hung over at church that day that he spent almost the entire time in the men's room, with a world-class headache and massive regret.

And when I got that opportunity in the advertising agency to step in for the ailing staff assistant, I proudly made a weekend visit home to show my parents my first (well-received) report. Dad's comment was, *I didn't know they let secretaries do that sort of thing.* I was crushed, and it was the last work-related project I ever shared.

On my first wedding day (there have only been two) Dad walked me out of the house before we left for church and told me that it was not too late to change my mind. On my second wedding day, he was distraught to see that I was actually wearing a wedding dress, thinking it was not appropriate.

Between my weddings, after I had broken off with a boyfriend and moved into my own apartment, my father begged me to not waste my money buying furniture because "my life was almost over already." I was 40 years old. I had never even owned my own bed.

When I was in my 30s, and published my first book, I invited him time after time to come to my readings.

Same with the three productions of my first play. He never came. In my 40s, I tricked him into seeing a rehearsal for my second play; he left after only a few minutes.

My only explanation for this is that he felt that I was overreaching. Becoming uppity. Thinking that I had something to say. Or maybe he was embarrassed for me. I never knew.

You see, in some ways, I simply had to choose. I had to create a new life for myself. Choose what kind of person I would become. Choose where my future would lie.

Soon after Tim gave me the gift of that first trip to Italy, I knew which direction I would take. I studied the language, dragged Tim around to different regions to explore the local culture and traditions, joined Italian organizations, made friends with Italians on the internet, wrote about Italy and, in 2014, we bought our first apartment in Sulmona. We did this with our friends Louis and Vicky, thanks to being "adopted" by an Abruzzese family and the extended community in our little city. Within seven years, we would all share ownership of the entire three-unit building.

Day by day, I am learning more about who I am and how I want to live in the world. And I am so grateful to everyone who has watched me take this journey and cheered me on.

Grazie.

Man on a Bicycle

I saw a man on Chestnut Street today
Wearing a blue short-sleeved cotton shirt
And baggy khaki cargo shorts
Riding an old fat-wheeled bicycle

His middle-aged frame was tan and a little sweaty
Despite the early hour; it would be hot today
His knees stuck out as he pedaled because
The bike was undeniably too short for him

My father looked the same way, riding
All those years ago back in Massapequa
Where we would journey off together, knees out
Like newborn giraffes, like unsteady colts

Conjuring, after summer dinners, the salt air and
sea as we
Headed for the beach to see Grandpa's
mosaics again on
The central mall and treat ourselves to a messy
ice cream roll
Before heading back home under our personal
twilight sky

Just Dad and me, and Grandpa, in his way
A visit to the ocean that brought him here
That brings us together in the end
Pedaling unsteadily between two worlds

Epilogue

Once upon a time, there was a group of 10 friends who asked me to plan a trip to Italy for them. It was – unbeknownst to any of us at the time – the beginning of Travel the Write Way, my tour company that brought small groups of visitors to Italy every year for more than ten years. They didn't care where they went, they just wanted to go to Italy with me and Tim.

I wrote to my friend Mario Scalzi who rented villas through his company, Parker Villas, and he said he had just the place. He said we should go to Abruzzo because it had the best food in Italy (*mi dispiace, Bologna*). Also, that the people were so friendly that some stranger was likely to come and invite us to dinner at their home. He said he could arrange for us to stay at a B&B in a town called Sulmona and that we would love it, not being traditional American tourists. We were a little more adventurous, and he thought we would really appreciate it.

After that, he said, we should go up to the northern-most part of Abruzzo to the little town of Civitella del Tronto, where he would arrange for first-class accommodations, a cooking class, a winery visit, and a tour of the local fortress — the last Bourbon outpost to surrender to the armies of the newly united Italy in 1861. So the 12 of us gathered in three cars and did just as he suggested. It was one of the best trips imaginable.

One of the must-see stops in the Sulmona area is the

Abbazia Morronese, the Abbey of the Holy Spirit, in nearby Badia. We all piled into the cars and drove ten minutes to the abbey; I asked for an English-speaking tour guide and out came a woman named Novelia to lead us around. Now, understand that Novelia was not a tour guide; she worked for the Italian government at several historic sites in Abruzzo, and she just happened to be in Badia the day we came. It was a day that changed our lives.

Novelia likes to say that she bewitched us, and it may be true. Later that evening, we met her and her sister, Vittoria, for drinks at the Hotel Ovidio in Sulmona. Within a few years, Tim and I and our two dear friends co-owned three apartments which had been restored to perfection by Vittoria's architect husband, Carlo. They are no more than 50 yards from the hotel we had drinks in that night.

We often ask ourselves: *How the hell did this happen?*

There's that bewitching thing, for sure, but the whole place is bewitching. Tucked into the beguiling Valley Peligna — less than two hours from Rome — surrounded by snow-capped mountains, Sulmona is a treasure. It is a little wild, geographically speaking, and maintains its deep traditions proudly.

With a history of earthquakes, floods, and invasions, Abruzzo has not always provided its inhabitants with an easy life. But these people are amazing, and that is what struck us. And yes, as soon as we arrived in Sulmona that first day, a local woman pulled my friend Vicky aside and asked where her people were from. She identified Vicky right away as Abruzzese. In fact, Vicky's mother was from a small village called Castel di Sangro, a 20-minute drive away. Her father was from Pescara. Abruzzese, through and through.

And to Mario's point, we have been invited for lunches and dinners and *aperitivi* countless times since settling in Sulmona.

In the early part of the 20th Century, the journalist and diplomat Primo Levi coined the phrase "*forte e gentile*" to describe the people of Abruzzo. Strong and gentle. Strong they would have to be. Gentle is what they are. Not that there aren't feuds, tempers, and disagreements. But we have been shown so much kindness and generosity by our Abruzzese friends that we have been made to feel a part of this crazy-wonderful extended family of Italians.

Surely, I am not Italian to these people; I will always be Italian American, and possibly even a little crazy for doing what I do. (Mario himself has called me mad as a hatter.)

But I have taken up the mantle of bringing Italy to anyone who will listen. In my tours I sought out the most provincial aspects of each city, large or small . . . regional cooking and wine experiences; small museums; meals with residents, sometimes even at their homes; Jewish history tours; classical concerts in villas; and introductions to locals wherever I could. I wanted my travelers to feel the same warm embrace that I have felt so many times as we explored this marvelous country.

Perhaps I am still searching for my roots. Like many other Italian Americans, I am doing what my father could not (or would not) do; or perhaps I am a little *pazza*, after all. Learning the language better is my first priority, but becoming more Italian in my soul is what I'm ultimately striving for.

For a balance somewhere between serenity and hysteria. In Abruzzo, I am surrounded by "*forte e gentile*." God willing, I will grow into that mindset before too long and that, to badly paraphrase Dante, the straight way will not be lost to me.

Buon viaggio!

Somewhere in Abruzzo

Somewhere
in the bulb of the red garlic
in the tiny green lentil
in the kernel of the wheat
in the musty truffle

Somewhere
in the rind of the fragrant cheese
in the pressed ripe olive
in the seeds of the pomegranate
in the skin of the grape

Somewhere
in all these things
you can lose your way
and never notice
until it is too late to ever go back

Acknowledgements

First, I want to thank Cavaliere Dianne Hales — author, journalist, and lover of the Italian language. I approached her before I got too far into this project and whined that I could think of no better title for it than the one she used for her blog. She graciously said I was free to use it. If you don't know Dianne's passionate approach to all things Italian, start by reading *La Bella Lingua.*

Hearty thanks to Barbara Worton, my oldest friend and writing partner in crime for so many decades I don't want to think about it. Knowing these stories almost as well as I do allowed her valuable insights and permission to cut, add, and critique that I would not grant to anyone else in the world.

Thanks to the travelers who trusted me to take them on worthwhile journeys – both literal and figurative – through Travel Italy the Write Way Tours and through my blog posts. Thank you for your patience, your enthusiasm and, most of all, your honesty. Sharing this important piece of my heart with you is the most gratifying thing I do.

Grazie to the entire province of Abruzzo and to all the incredible people in Sulmona who have adopted me. As a stranger in town you welcomed me, you endured my American-ness, you bewitched me, and you fed me. And you continue to feed me every day in more ways than you know.

Finally, thanks to Mario Scalzi, who convinced me to go to Sulmona all those years ago. And to Louis and Vicky and of course, my husband Tim, for making this incredible journey with me.

Because of you all, I have found the courage to claim the heritage of my father's family. Because of you all, I am becoming Italian.

All the Evidence Points to Something Else

Not the white Crisco in a can
Not the Velveeta brick in the frig
Not the crème de menthe parfait
Not the plastic-wrapped yellow cheese food product
Not the red gelatin dessert
Not the jar of Cheez Whiz
Not the super absorbent Wonder Bread
Nor the asparagus from the tall green and white can

None of these things said I was Italian

Not the orange spray cheese
Not the can of Spam
Not the dinners at the Chinese restaurant
Not the milk toast
Not the Rice Krispies
Not the savory meat
Not the Stern's pickles from big wooden barrels
Nor the frozen breaded fish sticks

How was I supposed to know?

O wretched Liederkranz!
O sweet Miracle Whip!
How was I supposed to know . . .?

About the Author

Linda Dini Jenkins is a writer, Italy tour planner, and Executive Director of the Pickering House in Salem, Massachusetts. She is also, happily, the Copy Editor of *Abruzzissimo Magazine*.

She is the author of two prior books: *Journey of a Returning Christian: Writing into God* and *Up at the Villa: Travels with my Husband.* Her poetry has been published in *VIA (Voices in Italian Americana), Ovunque Siamo, Vermont Voices, South Florida Poetry Review, Phoebe: A Journal of Feminist Scholarship Theory & Aesthetics, Poeti italo-americani e italo-canadesi, Tampa Review, Peregrine, Writer to Writer, Color Wheel/Mink Hills Journal, Bay Windows* and *Christmas Blessings.* She is the author of two plays: *Things I Never Told My Mother* and *If I'm Talking, Why Aren't You Listening?* co-written with Barbara Worton. She lives in Salem, Massachusetts and Sulmona, Italy with her husband Tim and their wonder poodle, Lexie.

Visit her website at *www.travelitalythewriteway.com* to learn more about her insane love for all things Italian as well as information about her holiday rental in Sulmona.

www.ingramcontent.com/pod-product-compliance
Lightning Source LLC
Chambersburg PA
CBHW051246020426
42333CB00025B/3080